Tourism Development

Tourism Development

Edited by

Nazmi Kozak and Metin Kozak

Cambridge
Scholars
Publishing

Tourism Development

Edited by Nazmi Kozak and Metin Kozak

This book first published 2015

Cambridge Scholars Publishing

Lady Stephenson Library, Newcastle upon Tyne, NE6 2PA, UK

British Library Cataloguing in Publication Data
A catalogue record for this book is available from the British Library

ISBN (10): 1-4438-7754-9
ISBN (13): 978-1-4438-7754-1

TABLE OF CONTENTS

INTRODUCTION

The development of tourism practices or operations is a dynamic activity: therefore, the process never stops. While one practice may become old–fashioned, an alternative may arise with a slightly or totally different understanding. As a continuous activity, the procedures of development require close cooperation as well as strong support from various government and non–government establishments, including local communities and tourism businesses. In all its forms and in every location, tourism develops on a sequential basis. The next step in tourism development rests upon the consequences, either positive or negative, of previous "lived experiences" as benefits or challenges for future generations. This means that what happened in the past could be a reason to take new action, either to maintain the sustainability of the earlier practice or to revisit the consequences of bad implementation.

In recent years, the issue of tourism development has been considered from a range of varying perspectives. For instance, Komppula (2014) has looked at the role of entrepreneurs in the development of competitiveness for rural destinations. Other research has focused on political stability and its possible influence on tourism development (e.g. Causevic & Lynch, 2013; Farmaki, Altinay, Botterill, & Hilke, 2015). The literature has also examined residents' attitudes and perceptions towards tourism development in their locations (e.g. Andereck & Vogt, 2000; Kim, Uysal, & Sirgy, 2012; Stylidis, Biran, Sit, & Szivas, 2014). In addition, empirical evidence also exists concerning the significance of community-based tourism in the development of viable strategies for tourism development in different respects (e.g. Halstead, 2003; López-Guzmán, Borges, & Hernandez-Merino, 2013; Tolkach & King, 2015).

Further, dating back to the 1980s, the literature has accommodated a wider range of reference books on tourism development, establishing a direct or indirect link with its supportive elements, such as sustainability (e.g. Kozak & Kozak, 2011; Sofield, 2003) and ecotourism (e.g. Fennell, 2007; Honey, 2008). There have been additional sources with a clear focus on the potential impacts of tourism development from social, economic, and environmental perspectives (e.g. Gartner, 1996: Mathieson & Wall, 1982). Also, Gartner (1996) has further advanced the debate on tourism development by including the planning of product development processes and implementation within tourism marketing. All of these issues have been considered across a large number of empirical studies conducted in both developed and developing countries over the past few decades.

In line with the coverage of the above remarks, this volume includes 12 studies from invited contributors. It has already become a traditional way of contributing to the existing body of tourism knowledge to select a group of papers presented at the *Interdisciplinary Tourism Research Conference* and *World Conference for Graduate Research in Tourism, Hospitality and Leisure* series, which take place bi-annually, each time in a different city in Turkey. The fourth series of these two conferences was successfully held in Istanbul on 4–9 June 2014, and attracted the participation of over 260 scholars worldwide. The cluster of papers included in this book address the issue of tourism development. The earlier collections released by Cambridge Scholars Publishing (CSP) have focused on different themes, such as sustainability (Kozak & Kozak, 2011), tourist behaviour (Kozak & Kozak, 2013a) and tourism research (Kozak & Kozak, 2013b).

The book is divided into two main parts.

The first five chapters in Part I focus, in large part, on the managerial side of sustainable tourism development. Chapter 1 presents local residents' perceptions of tourism development in Abu Dhabi, United Arab Emirates. Chapter 2 determines the economic aspects of how to preserve cultural landscapes for the sake of sustainable tourism development in Slovenia. Chapter 3 specifically examines the impact of community–based tourism applications, and identifies the most efficient ways to utilise community–based tourism in Vietnam. Chapter 4 identifies the salient stakeholders' features in the context of forestry–based ecotourism management in Malaysia. Along the same line, Chapter 5 is related to stakeholders, but develops an approach to stakeholder mapping as a tool for designing and implementing a tourism policy that generates a perfect environment and the incentives needed to improve the relationship between actors, contributing to the improvement of a destination management in Mexico. Chapter 6 focuses on the development of various strategies that will serve to achieve the vision of Dubai in 2020, and provides a partial SWOT analysis undertaken in this context.

The development of tourism practices also leads to the appearance of various new applications from one time period to another. For instance, until the early 1980s, worldwide debates on the development of tourism used to be dependent on individual tourists as backpackers, groups, or family visitors, travelling for the purpose of culture, nature, or adventure. However, there has been an enormous amount of debate concerning the side effects of mass tourism development, and many suggestions have been taken into account with regard to action needed to eliminate the influence of mass tourism, and to diversify the supply side, by developing different tourism products. Therefore, the six chapters in Part II deal with offering different forms of tourism products, on the basis of their current position in tourism development. Chapter 7 examines both sides of the human–environment relationship within the context of adventure tourism. Chapter 8 analyses the milestones in how ski resorts in France have progressed since the end of the 19th century. Chapter 9 has a specific focus on the development of rural tourism, and shows how Appreciative Inquiry is a helpful approach and an alternative research tool. Chapter 10 explores how medical tourism businesses that operate in Istanbul, Turkey, treat sustainability. Chapter 11 discusses the importance of coastal areas in the evolution of Villa Gesell, Argentina by applying the geo-historical method. Chapter 12 outlines a conceptual tourism collaboration approach modulated by the differing socio–economic and institutional rural settings of developed and developing countries.

Recognising tourism as a subject of academic investigation and taking tourism to have a worldwide focus, this book examines the subject of tourism development in detail, providing a list of specific case studies dealing with the tourism industries of various countries. The authors of the papers selected for inclusion in the book as potential chapters represent diverse locations, e.g. United Arab Emirates, Slovenia, Vietnam, Malaysia, Mexico, South Africa, France, Turkey, and Argentina. With their very strong sources and appeals in international tourism, these countries have all already become pioneers of the tourism and hospitality industry, or will do so in the future. The countries represented are also of value as unique destinations, with a varying quality or quantity of tourist attractions, e.g. human–made attractions in United Arab Emirates, and the mixed elements of both culture and nature in Vietnam, Argentina and South Africa, newly emerging exotic destinations that show promise for the future of tourism development at the international level. The remaining countries in the list are good examples of well–established and powerful international tourist destinations.

In short, there has been a greater focus on tourism development over the past few decades, not only within tourism but also from those studying in other fields, due to its extensive coverage of subjects ranging from psychology, sociology, planning, and marketing. Thus, this book encompasses a collection of chapters addressing various aspects of tourism development, varying from sustainability and ecotourism to cases of developing a range of alternative products. The contents of the chapters are enriched by selected practical case studies from a range of countries. The book is systematic in structure and thorough in content, and is useful for those in academia, as well as for those who wish to update their knowledge of tourism development and contribute to the ongoing research within the field.

Finally, we believe that as a reference book, this contribution will be a helpful resource, full of rich materials that refer to the applications of tourism development practices in worldwide case studies. The audience of this book may include advanced students of tourism, hospitality, leisure, recreation and economics, school libraries that have tourism, hospitality, leisure, recreation and economics programs, and practitioners (e.g. destination managers, ministry of tourism staff, individual tourism establishments). This book would serve as an excellent supplementary textbook for those examining the sustainability and the development of tourism, particularly in the context of such topics as tourism management, tourism economics, tourism geography, and tourism marketing.

Last but not least, we acknowledge and thank all the authors for their remarkable contributions and for showing the commitment and continuous cooperation that has been of such help in bringing this proposal to fruition. We would also like to thank Gözde Türktarhan Yılmazdoğan for her support to produce the subject index and *Cambridge Scholars Publishing* for giving us a unique opportunity to publish this volume in such a smooth and professional manner. Without your endless support, positivity and understanding, we would never have been able to make this happen.

Nazmi Kozak
Metin Kozak
The Editors

References

Andereck, K.L., & Vogt, C.A. (2000). The relationship between residents' attitudes toward tourism and tourism development options. *Journal of Travel Research*, 39(1), 27–36.

Causevic, S., & Lynch, P. (2013). Political (in)stability and its influence on tourism development. *Tourism Management, 34,145-157.*

Farmaki, A., Altinay, L., Botterill, D., & Hilke, S. (2015). Politics and sustainable tourism: the case of Cyprus. *Tourism Management,* 47, 178-190.

Fennell, D. (2007). *Ecotourism*, 3rd edition, Oxon: Routledge.

Honey, M. (2008) *Ecotourism and sustainable development*, 2nd edition, Washington: Island Press.

Gartner, W.C. (1996). *Tourism development: principles, processes and policies*. New York: John Wiley.

Halstead, L. (2003). *Making community-based tourism work: an assessment of factors contributing to successful community-owned tourism development in Caprivi, Namibia.* Windhoek: DEA Publications.

Kim, K., Uysal, M., & Sirgy, M.J. (2012). How does tourism in a community impact the quality of life of community residents?. *Tourism Management*, 36, 527–540.

Komppula, R. (2014). The role of individual entrepreneurs in the development of competitiveness for a rural tourism destination – a case study. *Tourism Management,* 40, 361-371.

Kozak, M., & Kozak, N. (eds., 2013a). *Aspects of tourist behavior.* Newcastle upon Tyne: Cambridge Scholars Publishing.

Kozak, N., & Kozak, M. (eds., 2013b). *Tourism research: an interdisciplinary perspective.* Newcastle upon Tyne: Cambridge Scholars Publishing.

Kozak, M., & Kozak, N. (eds., 2011). *Sustainability of tourism: cultural and environmental perspectives.* Newcastle upon Tyne: Cambridge Scholars Publishing.

López-Guzmán, T., Borges, O., & Hernandez-Merino, M. (2013). Analysis of community-based tourism in Cape Verde – a study on the island of São Vicente. *Anatolia*, 24(2), 129-143.

Mathieson, A., & Wall, G. (1982). *Tourism, economic, physical and social impacts*. London: Longman.

Tolkach, D., & King, B. (2015). Strengthening community-based tourism in a new resource-based island nation: why and how?. *Tourism Management*, 48, 386-398.

Sofield, T.H.B. (2003). *Empowerment for sustainable tourism development*. Bingley: Emerald.

Stylidis, D., Biran, A., Sit, J., & Szivas, E.M. (2014). Residents' support for tourism development: the role of residents' place image and perceived tourism impacts. *Tourism Management*, 45, 260-274.

CHAPTER ONE

PERCEPTIONS OF LOCAL RESIDENTS IN ABU DHABI TOWARDS THE DEVELOPMENT OF TOURISM

GORDANA KOVJANIC

Abstract

This chapter presents the perceptions that local residents have towards the development of tourism in Abu Dhabi. As a new industry in a predominantly oil-based economy, tourism brings new opportunities and new challenges to all stakeholders. To prosper, tourism needs support from local residents. Consequently, their attitudes should be taken into consideration in any future tourism planning. A Principal Component Analysis was used to identify five domains around which local residents' perceptions with respect to tourism were formed. These five domains were used in regression analyses to examine the effects various independent variables have on the local residents' attitudes. **Keywords:** residents' attitudes, tourism development, Abu Dhabi.

1.1. Introduction

Commercial exploitation of oil in the UAE has brought dramatic changes to what was one of the poorest regions of the world, and has transformed this country into a rich, modern society in a mere 40 years. The oil industry has brought progress and wealth to the country, but the UAE government is also aware of the need for economic diversification. Abu Dhabi's official development strategy, *Abu Dhabi Vision 2030* (2008), aims not just to diversify the economy but also to change the image of the country. The development of new sectors within the economy has made the UAE, and particularly Abu Dhabi, a more attractive destination for tourists. The UAE also provides a comfortable living environment for its residents, in spite of the harsh natural environment found in the country. The current socio-cultural environment allows for the co–existence of the old and the modern, the traditional and the technological. The strategic decision of the Abu Dhabi government to develop cultural tourism has two dimensions. The first dimension is aimed at preserving the local Bedouin heritage and traditions, both in their tangible and intangible form. The second dimension is aimed at accessing global markets, attracting diverse peoples to visit the country, and spreading knowledge and culture through new developments, such as the Guggenheim Museum and the Louvre Museum on Saadiyat Island.

1.2. Literature Review

The theoretical framework that is used in this chapter is based on (i) Doxy's 'Irridex' model (as cited in Mason, 2008), (ii) Butler's (1980) 'Tourism Area Life Cycle' and, (iii) Ap's (1990) 'Social Exchange Theory'. All of these models have been previously implemented in different geographical locations. Notwithstanding this, the assumptions, principles, and even the limitations that were identified in these seminal works formed the theoretical foundation of much subsequent research, most of which included measurement of local residents' perceptions of and attitudes towards tourism development and its impact. The significance of this impact lies in the connection between the development of tourism and the (perceived) quality of the local residents' lives. Results suggest that tourism activity is an important factor in determining the quality of life in many local communities, and is a factor in stimulating social prosperity (Crouch & Ritchie, 1999).

Most previous research on the impact of tourism has included the measurement of the local residents' perceptions and attitudes towards the development of tourism and the influence that tourism has on their lives. The identification of these influences has gained more importance since the discovery that they are intimately connected with the quality of the local community's life. For example, when a destination's potential to provide a high standard of living for local residents is taken into account, researchers have demonstrated that tourism activity is an important factor in determining the quality of life for many local communities since tourism stimulates social prosperity (Crouch & Ritchie, 1999).

The research aim of the present empirical study, conducted between 2011–2013, was to answer the following research questions:

- What are the Abu Dhabi local residents' perceptions of the impact of tourism development in the emirate?
- What are the relationships between the selected determinants and underlying dimensions that explain perceived tourism impact?
- What are the perceptual differences among different groups of residents (if any such perceptual differences exist)?

The present chapter discusses the findings of an investigation into the first two questions, but it does not deal with the statistical analysis and results that are related to the third research question. The research that I conducted in the emirate of Abu Dhabi includes an examination of several socio-demographic variables as well as a number of behavioural variables that are related to the respondents' experience of tourism within the emirate. This paper focuses on eight variables that have been selected from a total of 18 variables that were examined. These include:

- number of foreign destinations that were visited by the respondent,
- frequency of foreign travel,
- frequency of contacts with tourists,
- frequency of communication with tourists,
- distance to the nearest tourist attraction,
- knowledge of local history and heritage,
- perception of the rising number of tourists in a particular destination,
- number of tourism professionals known by the respondent.

Some of the variables that are mentioned above (for example, 'the distance to the nearest tourist attraction', and 'frequency of contact with tourists') have been used in previous research. However, some of the other variables, such as 'knowledge of local history and heritage', and 'perception of the rising number of tourists in a particular destination' have not been used in previous research. These variables were chosen by the researcher based on the researcher's extensive experience living in the emirate, and observing tourism practices.

Results from previous studies indicate that residents who have more contacts with tourists hold negative perceptions of tourism development (Fredline & Faulkner, 2000; Williams & Lawson, 2001). However, we also find studies that show the opposite finding; residents who have more contact with tourists hold positive perceptions of tourism (Akis *et al.* 1996; Jackson & Inbakaran, 2006).

Previous research suggests that the distance to the nearest tourist attraction can also determine local residents' attitudes towards tourism development (Jurowski & Gursoy, 2004). Some studies conclude that people who reside close to tourist zones have more positive attitudes towards tourism development (Belisle & Hoy, 1980; Mansfeld & Ginosar, 1994; Sheldon & Var, 1984). But again, we can also find studies that indicate that people who reside close to tourist zones have more negative attitudes towards the impact of tourism development (Madrigal, 1995; Williams & Lawson, 2001).

In early research on attitudes towards tourism, knowledge of tourism and the local economic situation were considered to be determinants with respect to residents' perceptions of tourism development (Davis *et al.,* 1988; Lankford, 1994). Because tourism is a new industry in Abu Dhabi that employs only about 1% of local residents, and because the local people do not know much about tourism, the present study includes another variable, namely, 'knowledge of local history and heritage'. Abu Dhabi emirate is considered to be one of the wealthiest countries in the world, and its residents enjoy one of the most advanced social welfare programs in the world. As a consequence of this, many local residents do not to give much thought to economic issues. To illustrate the privileged position of the local residents, H.H. Sheikh Khalifa, the country's president, cancelled local resident (Emirati) bank debts in 2011 to celebrate 40 years of statehood, while much of the rest of the world was struggling through a financial crisis (UAE National Media Council, 2014).

Previous research has not considered residents' perceptions of the increasing number of tourists in a destination from year to year as a determinant with respect to their attitude towards the development of tourism. It was decided to include this variable in the present study, while acknowledging that the lifestyle and general practices of Emiratis (particularly the female population who constitute 48.8% of the sample included) is to avoid contact with foreigners in public places. According to local social norms, Emirati females avoid communication with strangers, especially males. Notwithstanding this, a rising or declining number of tourists may be perceived visually, without any direct contact between the local resident and the tourist, so it was deemed appropriate to include this variable in the study.

Examining determinants such as 'the frequency of the local residents' foreign travel' and 'the number of foreign destinations that the local resident has visited' gives us insight into the personal experiences of tourism among residents. However, these determinants have not been extensively used in similar studies. Inclusion of these determinants in the present study was based on the hypothesis that residents who had more travel experience abroad and consequently possessed more knowledge about tourism in general, would hold different perceptions about tourism development in their own country when compared with residents with little or no travel experience.

1.3. Methodology

Data for this study were collected using a survey method in different locations in Abu Dhabi emirate, during 2011/2012. The instrument that was used in the study contained two sections. The first section concentrated on the socio-demographic characteristics of the respondents, and the second section contained a number of statements that were used to assess the respondents' perceptions of the impact that tourism has in their area. 55 statements, derived from my study of the relevant literature, were adapted to the local situation and included in the questionnaire. Participants were asked to rate each statement on a five point Likert-type scale, where the value of '(1)' represented a negative response (strongly disagree) and the value of '(5)' represented a favourable response (strongly agree). The instrument was originally written in English and then translated into Arabic, and the initial questionnaire was pre-tested on a sample of 87 local residents of Al Ain (a city in Abu Dhabi emirate). In order to obtain a basic set of variables, a principal component analysis was performed. The factor structure that emerged from the principle component analysis was used for the construction of the final instrument. This work resulted in a new questionnaire that contained 28 statements that included items with factor loadings of more than .5 about the possible impact of tourism. This new instrument was distributed across the Abu Dhabi emirate during the autumn and winter of 2012. The reliability of the questionnaire was calculated by using an arithmetical coefficient, Cronbach's alpha. The results showed that the value of Cronbach's alpha coefficient for all of the items that were included in the questionnaire was .791. This indicates that the questionnaire was sufficiently reliable to measure the variables that were identified in the study.

The study sample consisted of 535 residents from three administrative parts of Abu Dhabi emirate: Al Ain, Al Gharbia, and Abu Dhabi city. The target group for this study consisted exclusively of Abu Dhabi nationals. Fortunately, a convenient sample of individuals was available and willing to participate in the study. There were slightly more males (51%) than females (49%) in the sample. A majority of the participants were aged 25 to 34 years, comprising more than one third of the total number of respondents. More than two thirds of the 535 respondents had no professional relationship with the tourism industry. They see Abu Dhabi as a new, fresh, and distinct destination (mean value of item 4.68), in which their identity and cultural pride can blossom (mean value of item 4.26).

A promax rotated principal component analysis was also used on the 28 items (on the sample of 535 residents) to identify general groups of attitudes towards tourism in Abu Dhabi. The Kaiser-Meyer-Olkin Measure of Sampling Adequacy was .868, and the Burtlett test of Sphericity showed significance on the .001 level, thus indicating that the data was suitable for a factor analysis. A cut-off point of .5 was used to include items in the interpretation of a particular factor. All of the factor loadings were inspected, and items that either loaded on several factors or had low loadings were deleted. After several iterations of the factor analysis, a clear five factor solution was achieved, which explained 54.3% of the variance. The five factors were labelled as: (i) *negative effects of tourism*, (ii) *positive effects of tourism*, (iii) *support for the development of tourism*, (iv) *features of tourist destination*, and (v) *perceptions of tourist behaviour*. The five conceptually meaningful domains that emerged from the factor analysis were tested for reliability by using Cronbach's Alpha coefficients. The coefficients ranged from a high of .89 (domain 1), to a low of .65 (domain 4), as presented in Table 1.1. I decided to use five conceptually consistent factor solutions, and factor scores were calculated for subsequent analysis. Later, in the subsequent regression analyses, these factor scores were used as dependent variable measures to examine the effects of various independent variables on the residents' attitudes.

Table 1.1 – Results of factor analysis

Extracted factors	Eigenvalues	% of variance explained	Cronbach α	Mean	Standard deviation
F1 – *Negative effects of tourism*	6.60	23.57	.89	3.38	.88
F2 - *Positive effects of tourism*	4.13	14.74	.70	3.76	.80
F3 - *Support for the development of tourism*	1.83	6.53	.74	4.15	.71
F4 - *Features of tourist destination*	1.44	5.13	.65	4.52	.45
F5 - *Perceptions of tourist behaviours*	1.20	4.30	.79	2.88	1.01

1.4. Results

To examine the relationship between the selected determinants and the underlying dimensions of perceived tourism impact, I performed a series of multiple regression analyses. The following determinants were considered as independent variables: (i) the number of foreign destinations visited, (ii) frequency of foreign travel, (iii) frequency of contact with tourists, (iv) frequency of communication with tourists, (v) distance to the nearest tourist attraction, (vi) knowledge of local history and heritage, (vii) perception of the rising number of tourists in a destination, and (viii) the number of tourism professionals known by the respondent. Five factors were identified as the result of the factor analysis and were consequently considered to be dependent variables. The findings are as follows:

- The multiple regression analysis of the relationship between the determinants and a perceived negative impact of tourism indicated that a correlation exists between these variables. There was only one determinant, namely 'the number of foreign destinations visited', that had a significant effect on the perceived negative impact, with 3.8% (R^2) of variance at a level of p=.006. Respondents who had more travel experience were less inclined to have a negative view of the impact of tourism development.
- The multiple regression analysis of the relationship between the determinants and the perceived positive effects of tourism revealed a statistical correlation. Three determinant variables were perceived as having a significant influence on positive effects, namely, 'the frequency of contact with tourists', 'the distance to the nearest tourist attraction', and 'knowledge of local history and heritage'; explaining 12.1% (R^2) of variance at a level of p=.026. Consequently, we claim that residents who have a wider knowledge of local history and heritage and who have encountered tourists more frequently recognize the positive impact of tourism. In addition, residents who live far away from tourist attractions were observed as holding less positive views on tourism.
- The multiple regression analysis of the relationship between the determinants and an overall support for tourism development did not show any statistically significant relationship. As a result, none of selected determinants were likely to influence the residents' support.

- The multiple regression analysis of the relationship between the determinants and tourists' perceived behaviour revealed a statistically significant correlation. There were three determinant variables that had significant effects on the perception of tourist behaviour, namely, 'the number of foreign destinations previously visited', 'frequency of foreign travel, and 'frequency of contact with tourists', with 3.4% (R^2) of variance on a level of p=.014, p=.042, and p=.027, respectively. Respondents who had visited several destinations abroad and who often encountered tourists were observed as possessing fewer negative views on the behaviour of tourists. Locals who frequently travel abroad have a more sensitive perception of the behaviour of tourists.
- The multiple regression analysis of the relationship between the determinants and the positive features of a destination revealed a statistical correlation. There were four determinant variables that had significant effects on the perception of a destination's features, namely, (i) the distance to the nearest tourist attraction, (ii) an awareness of the rising number of tourists in a destination from year to year, (iii) frequency of contact with tourists and, most particularly, (iv) knowledge of local history and heritage, with 12% (R^2) of variance on a level of p=.002, p=.012, p=.021, and p=.000, respectively. Residents who perceived an increasing number of tourists, who communicated with them frequently, and who had a profound knowledge of local history and heritage, were also found to be more aware of the positive features of the destination. In contrast, those who lived at a greater distance from tourist attractions were more likely to have a negative perspective of the features of the destination.

From the results that were obtained by the multiple regression analyses, it can be concluded that the selected variables explained just 31.3% of variance in the attitudes of the local residents towards the development of tourism in Abu Dhabi. Obviously, there exist variables which were not considered in this study, but seem to play a significant role in the formation of Abu Dhabi nationals' perceptions of tourism. There are a number of characteristics of the local residents and their lifestyle that should be identified and be included in subsequent research. The residents' religion, traditions, tribal past, and the dynamics of their social structure, along with other socio-economic factors, are possible variables that should be considered in future research.

1.5. Discussion

A review of the available literature indicates that tourism development in Abu Dhabi in general, (and more specifically from the point of view of the local residents), has not been subject to previous academic study. The only academic article that is thematically related to this study examined the challenges of economic diversification through tourism, using Abu Dhabi as a case-study (Sharply, 2002).

The support of the local population for and their attitudes towards the development of tourism are crucial for the long term success of the tourism industry. When residents take note of new employment opportunities, new shopping facilities and restaurants, new cultural, artistic and recreational facilities, they are more likely to have positive attitudes towards tourism. With their support, the tourism industry has a better chance to succeed (Andriotis & Vaughan, 2003).

The tourism industry, as a part of Abu Dhabi's new economy, is one of the key drivers behind economic diversification (*Abu Dhabi Vision 2030*). Abu Dhabi is targeting the upper market segments in the development of luxury and cultural tourism, and is focusing on cultivating a more exclusive niche in the tourism market which is distinct from its more famous neighbour, Dubai. Major investment in tourism infrastructure and facilities has initiated a number of radical changes in both the natural and social environment. The new Abu Dhabi Tourism and Culture Authority is actively promoting Abu Dhabi as a tourist destination overseas, and has organized different events to attract tourists to the emirate. A study of Abu Dhabi residents' opinions and perceptions in the first phase of Abu Dhabi's destination life cycle has revealed five underlying dimensions of the perceived impact of tourism. Understanding these dimensions may assist decision-makers in their strategic planning of tourism development.

The results of the study show that the frequency of contacts with tourists determined the attitude of residents towards the behaviour of visiting tourists, the features of the destination, and the perceived positive impact of tourism. Residents who encountered tourists more often were less likely to observe the tourists' negative behaviour. Residents were also more aware of the features of the tourist destination, and had a more positive attitude towards the development of local tourism, in general. The more they were exposed to the positive impact of tourism and interaction with tourists, the more favourable was the residents' attitude. That means that the development of local tourism in Abu Dhabi is in the first phase, the so called "welcoming phase", in which negative feelings among residents are not in evidence (Akis, Peristianis, & Warner, 1996). This is in agreement with the conclusions that other researchers have reached – that residents who meet more tourists have more positive opinions on the impact that tourism has on the life of the local community, its image, and its economy (Andereck *et al.*, 2005).

The distance to the nearest tourist attraction is a variable that affects the attitude of residents towards the positive effects of tourism and the features of Abu Dhabi as a tourist destination. The more distant residents are from tourist sites, the less likely they are to observe the positive features of a destination, and the more likely they are to have a negative view of tourism. Previous research has shown that when the residents' distance from tourist areas increases, negative reactions towards further tourism development increase as well (Belisle & Hoy, 1980; Besculides *et al.*, 2002; Fredline & Faulkner, 2000; Weaver & Lawton, 2001; Williams & Lawson, 2001).

Knowledge of local history and heritage proved to be an important determinant with respect to the local residents' viewpoints on the positive impact of tourism and the destination's features. Residents with a wider knowledge of local history and heritage held more favourable opinions on the positive features of the destination and the impact of tourism development in Abu Dhabi. This variable was selected based on personal experience in vocational tourism education in Abu Dhabi, and the conclusion that local residents tend to have a limited awareness of tourism. Previous studies have used 'knowledge of tourism' as a variable and have concluded that individuals who have knowledge about tourism were more aware of the positive impact of tourism on life in their local community (Lankford & Howard, 1994), its image and economy, but not on the environment and public services in the destination (Andereck *et al.*, 2005).

The residents' experience of being tourists themselves, measured by the number of foreign destinations that they had previously visited and frequency of foreign travel proved to be an important determinant with respect to their disposition towards the development of local tourism. Respondents who had visited several foreign destinations held less negative views on aspects of tourists' behaviour in public, and on the impact of tourism development. More than one third (35%) of the respondents had visited only one foreign region, almost a quarter (24%) of respondents had visited two regions of the world, one fifth (20%) of respondents had visited three different regions, and around one fifth of respondents had visited four or more regions of the world. The most-visited region among respondents was the GCC region (80%). It should be noted that the majority of visitors to Abu Dhabi come from the GCC region (*Abu Dhabi TCA Statistics*, 2013). On the other hand, Abu Dhabi residents who travelled abroad more frequently had a better perception of the behaviour of incoming visitors in their home country. Approximately 75% of the respondents said they rarely travelled abroad (1-2 times per year or less), 12% of respondents travelled abroad three times a year, 5% of respondents travelled abroad four times a year, and 7% of respondents travelled abroad more than four times a year. The present study found that residents with limited experience of tourism had more concerns about the social impact of tourism development. Wider personal experience of tourism was found to open the minds of individuals and contribute to higher levels of tolerance towards visitors from different cultural backgrounds and lifestyles, as one might expect.

The perceptions of local residents of the rising number of tourists in Abu Dhabi from year to year determined their perspective on tourism development. The majority of the respondents were aware of the fact that more visitors are coming from abroad; 57% noticed much more tourists than before, 32% noticed more tourists than before, 7% noticed no difference, and 3% believed there are fewer tourists than before. Abu Dhabi nationals are a minority in their own country, and tend not to mix with expats, who comprise 80% of population. Those who correctly recognized the rising number of tourists from year to year were also more able to identify the positive features of the destination; especially newly-developed tourism infrastructure and facilities, recently built attractions, and public events that combine to make Abu Dhabi more attractive as a destination.

1.6. Conclusion

According to the findings of this study, the perceptions of Abu Dhabi's local residents towards the development of tourism are formed around five underlying dimensions; namely, the negative impact of tourism, the positive impact of tourism, support for the development of tourism, features of the tourist destination, and perceptions of the tourists' behaviour. Correlations between predictor variables and selected criteria revealed statistically significant contributions of several variables; namely, frequency of contact with tourists, distance to the nearest tourist attraction, knowledge of local history and heritage, residents' tourism experience, and residents' perception of the increasing number of visitors to Abu Dhabi.

Abu Dhabi should invest more in promotional activities inside the country to familiarize the local people with tourism and its importance. Emiratis are traditionally hospitable and welcoming to all guests, but they are a minority in their own country, and they do not mix a great deal with strangers. The knowledge of local traditions and heritage, as well as the frequency of contact with tourists should be encouraged. It is important to make prerequisites for interactions between tourists and locals, and to cultivate their mutual contact and communication. The opening up of the local community is of great importance for the continuing improvement and development of tourism. This should be done with respect for traditional values, life-styles, and local customs and habits, so as to embrace the positive contribution that the local residents can make to tourism.

References

Abu Dhabi Government (2008). *Abu Dhabi Economic Vision 2030.* Abu Dhabi: Author. Retrieved from: https://www.ecouncil.ae/PublicationsEn/economic-vision-2030-full-versionEn.pdf

Abu Dhabi Tourism and Culture Authority Statistics (2013). *Abu Dhabi Tourism and Culture Authority* (Brochure). Abu Dhabi: Author

Akis, S., Peristianis, N., & Warner, J. (1996). Residents' attitudes to tourism development: the case of Cyprus. *Tourism Management, 17* (17), 481-494.

Andereck, K.L., Valentine, K.M., Knopf, R.C., & Vogt, C.A. (2005). Residents' perceptions of community tourism impacts. *Annals of Tourism Research*, *32* (4), 1056-1076.

Andriotis, K., & Vaughan, D.R. (2003). Urban residents' attitudes towards tourism development: The case of Crete. *Journal of Travel Research, 42* (2), 172-185.

Ap, J. (1990). Residents' perceptions research on the social impacts of tourism. *Annals of Tourism Research, 17* (4), 610-616.

—. (1992). Residents' perceptions on tourism impacts. *Annals of Tourism Research*, *19*(4), 665-690.

Ap, J., & Crompton, J.L. (1993). Residents' strategies for responding to tourism impacts. *Journal of Travel Research, 32* (1), 47-50.

Ap, J., & Crompton, J.L. (1998). Developing and testing a tourism impact scale. *Journal of Travel Research, 37* (2), 120-130.

Belisle, F.J., & Hoy, D.R. (1980). The perceived impact of tourism by residents: A case study of Santa Marta, Columbia, *Annals of Tourism Research, 7* (1), 83-101.

Besculides, A., Lee, M.E., & McCormick, P.J. (2002). Residents' perceptions of the cultural benefits of tourism. *Annals of Tourism Research, 29* (2), 303-319.

Butler, R.W. (1980). The concept of a tourism area cycle of evolution: Implications for the management of resources, *Canadian Geographer, 24* (1), 5-12.

Crouch, G.I., & Ritchie, J.R.B. (1999). Tourism, competitiveness and societal prosperity. *Journal of Business Research, 44* (3), 137-152.

Davidson, C. (2009). Abu Dhabi's new economy: Oil, investment and domestic development. *Middle East Policy, 16* (2), 59-79.

Davis, D., Allen, J., Cosenza, R.M. (1988). Segmenting local residents by their attitudes, interest, and opinions toward Tourism. *Journal of Travel Research, 27* (2), 2-8.

Fredline, E., & Faulkner, B. (2000). Host community reactions - A cluster analysis. *Annals of Tourism Research, 27* (3), 763-784.

Gursoy, D., Jurowski, C., & Uysal, M. (2002). Resident attitudes: A structural modelling approach. *Annals of Tourism Research, 29*(1), 231-264.

Gursoy, D., & Rutherford, D. (2004). Host attitudes towards tourism: An improved structural model. *Annals of Tourism Research, 31*(3), 495-516.

Gursoy, D., Chi, C.G., & Dyer, P. (2009). An examination of locals' attitudes. *Annals of Tourism Research, 36*(4), 723-726.

Haralambopoulos, N., & Pizam, A. (1996). Perceived impacts of tourism: The case of Samos. *Annals of Tourism Research, 23*(3), 503-526.

Harrill, R., & Potts, T.D. (2003). Tourism planning in historic districts: Attitudes toward tourism development in Charleston. *Journal of the American Planning Association, 69*(3), 233-244.

Jackson, M.S., & Inbakaran, R.J. (2006). Evaluating residents' attitudes and intentions to act towards tourism development in regional Victoria, Australia. *International Journal of Tourism Research, 8*, 355-366.

Jurowski, C., & Gursoy, D. (2004). Distance effects on residents' attitudes toward tourism. *Annals of Tourism Research, 31*(2), 296-312.

Jurowski, C., Uysal, M., & Williams, D.R. (1997). A theoretical analysis of host community resident reactions to tourism. *Journal of Travel Research, 36*(2), 3-11.

Lankford, S. (1994). Attitudes and perceptions toward tourism and rural regional development. *Journal of Travel Research, 33*(4), 35-43.

Lankford, S., & Howard, R.D. (1994). Developing a tourism impact attitude scale. *Annals of Tourism Research, 21*(1), 121-139.

Madrigal, R. (1995). Residents' perceptions and the role of government. *Annals of Tourism Research, 22*(1), 86-102.

Mansfeld, Y., & Ginosar, O. (1994). Determinants of locals' perceptions and attitudes towards tourism development in their locality. *Geoforum, 25*(2), 227-248.

Mason, P. (2008). *Tourism impacts, planning and management* (2nd ed.). Oxford: Elsevier.

Sharpley, R. (2008). The challenges of economic diversification through tourism: the case of Abu Dhabi. *International Journal of Tourism Research, 4*, 221-235.

Sheldon, P.J., & Var, T. (1984). Residents' attitudes to tourism in North Wales. *Tourism Management, 5*, 40-47.

UAE National Media Council. (2014). UAEinteract: Khalifa bin Zayed: Generous historical leadership in building national pride and achieving happiness and well-being of citizens. Retrieved from: http://www.uaeinteract.com/docs/Khalifa_bin_Zayed_Generous_histor ical_leadership_in_building_national_pride_and_achieving_happiness _and_well-being_of_citizens/59164.htm

Weaver, D.B., & Lawton, L.J. (2001). Resident perceptions in the urban-rural fringe. *Annals of Tourism Research, 28*(2), 439-458.

Williams, J., & Lawson, R. (2001). Community issues and resident opinions of tourism. *Annals of Tourism Research, 28*(2), 269-290.

CHAPTER TWO

ECONOMIC ASPECTS OF PRESERVING TRADITIONAL CULTURAL LANDSCAPES FOR SUSTAINABLE TOURISM DEVELOPMENT

MIHA MARKELJ AND GORDANA IVANKOVIČ

Abstract

This chapter introduces a new interdisciplinary methodological approach in tourism and landscape studies for determining the economic aspects of preserving traditional cultural landscapes for sustainable tourism development in the upper part of the Selščica valley, Slovenia. The research nests on the definition that the traditional cultural landscape is a depiction of natural and traditional cultural elements that give the landscape its distinguishing features. Results provide a significant contribution to the already existing approaches in sustainable tourism development and planning, since the concrete example under study is seen to carry a wider applicability. **Keywords:** interdisciplinary approach, sustainable tourism, tourism development, cultural landscape, Slovenia.

2.1. Introduction

Cultural landscapes are spaces of rich natural and cultural diversity that are often perceived through the imaginative lens as spaces of fairy tales and fables. Careful analysis of their natural and cultural elements, however, enables us to understand their value, for which it is essential to protect and preserve them. Despite the huge symbolic, socio–economic, cultural as well as natural importance they represent a fragile eco–system that cannot exist as such without a balanced and sustainable development.

We need to acknowledge the fact that in the eyes of the general public, cultural landscapes are still seen to be places with low income value that do not contribute to the welfare of the local community. However, the fact remains that different eco–systems provide a large variety of services that are of significant value (Ruzzier, Žujo, Marinšek, & Sosič, 2010).

The development of modern technology, population growth and the processes of globalization have had a major impact on the environment with largely negative consequences. In the past, the effects of various environmental projects were only rarely thought over or taken into consideration. The experts did not at all examine their long–term economic consequences for the field of cultural landscape preservation.

With this particular orientation, our research focuses on the upper part of an alpine valley in Slovenia with its narrow gorges and picturesque villages sitting atop the mountain slopes that have preserved their hundred year–old traditions and whose cultural landscape has been left more or less intact. This is very important since it allows us to determine and emphasize the economic aspects that can be gained from preserving this traditional cultural landscape for future sustainable tourism development.

2.2. Literature Review

To determine the economic aspects and to measure the value of natural and cultural heritage in the field of tourism, a variety of methods and methodological approaches are available[1]. These have been described or showcased, directly or indirectly, in numerous publications and studies since the first notable publications tried to determine the value of natural and cultural heritage at the end of the 20th century[2], when the awareness of uncontrolled exploitation of natural and cultural resources reached a critical point (Pearce & Moran, 1994; Pearce & Turner, 1990, 1992). One of the most influential publications of that time is the book entitled *Economic Valuation of the Environment* by Garrod and Willis (1999) that provided a reader–friendly examination of the major techniques used to evaluate environmental goods and services.

Later publications such as *Assessing the Economic Value of Ecosystem Conservation* (Pagiola, Ritter, & Bishop, 2004), *Valuing our Natural Environment* (Ozdemiroglu, Tinch, Johns, Provins, Powell, & Twiggers-Ross, 2006) and *Pricing Nature* by Hanley, Barbier and Barbier (2009) have all contributed significantly to improvements in techniques and methodological approaches, and have since been taken into account also by the local researchers of the environment in Slovenia (Ruzzier *et al.,* 2010; Verbič & Slabe, 2004, 2007). However, it has to be stated that the above–mentioned methodological approaches tend to represent complex research methods as well as difficult and time–consuming data acquisition, but most of all; they are intended for research on larger and well–known tourist destinations and thus cannot be applied to small and not yet developed tourist areas.

2.3. Methodology

This chapter thus introduces a new interdisciplinary methodological approach that primarily identifies the traditional elements within a cultural landscape and combines them according to accurate historical data and modern day cartographic material in order to recognize their modifications in the past and to accurately position them with regard to the present time. After thus establishing the primary research field we go on to identify direct/short-term and indirect/long-term economic benefits of restoring the traditional cultural landscape.

This is then applied to the protected cultural landscape in the upper part of the Selščica valley in Slovenia, with a view of presenting real direct and indirect economic aspects and benefits that the local population and the regional government could benefit from. The results are also then combined with the results from a pilot research project that was carried out in Tuscany by Filippo Randelli and his colleagues from the Department of Economic Sciences at the University of Florence to highlight the possibilities for sustainable tourism development in the future.

2.4. Results

The cultural landscape of the upper part of the Selščica valley contains a large variety of Tyrolean cultural elements. These are remnants of the medieval "Freising colonization"[3] dating back to the 13th century. Elements of that period include architectural heritage, the Tyrolean dialect, specific customs and traditions as well as particular knowledge and skills that were developed as a result of the harsh living conditions on steep mountain slopes and ridges.

In the case of the upper Selščica valley, it has been shown that several factors have contributed to the changing of the Tyrolean heritage (Markelj, 2009). The ones with the most impact can be categorized as reforms of Maria Theresa and Emperor Franz Joseph (namely fiscal, educational and economic reforms at the beginning of the 19th century) and later emigration to urban centres and depopulation, which gradually led to uncontrolled natural reforestation of the land surfaces.

It has been established that the reforestation is the most evident in the upper part of the Selščica valley alongside some other cultural landscape spaces in Slovenia (Kobler, 2001). For that reason we analysed the

Franciscan land cadaster map from 1825[4], because it represents the most reliable source and gives the most accurate data, but also because it shows the landscape of the upper part of the valley before the major changes occurred.

While it has been established that the cultural landscape has changed primarily due to the reforestation, other analyses have been carried out to determine if the same can be said about the cultural heritage. Previous research has shown that regardless of the changes taking place in the natural environment (Markelj, 2011b, 2012); these did not have a significant impact on the changes that occurred in the field of cultural heritage.[5] The research thus primarily focuses on identifying individual land units that have been overgrown with forests in the time period between 1825 and 2013.

Based on the primary data that can be obtained from the interactive map of the Register of Slovene cultural heritage (2013) that gives us an insight into the fragmented overview of Franciscan cadaster, and based on the interactive territorial map of Slovenia (Figure 2.1) that allows the possibility of calculating the surface area of each significant land unit and displays its cadaster numbers, we had the possibility to accurately detect the units that have been overgrown with forests.

Figure 2.1 – Interactive territorial map of Slovenia.

The total equivalent of forest and non–forest cadastral units in the year 2013, if we look back at 1825 for the village communities in the upper part of the Selščica valley, is 7.7568 hectares in total. Individual village communities make up 3.0035 hectares in the villages of Zgornje Danje and Spodnje Danje, 2.6748 hectares in the village of Ravne, 1.5489 hectares in the village of Zabrdo, 1.1901 in the village of Zali Log, and -0.6605 hectares[6] in the villages of Zgornja Sorica and Spodnja Sorica.

In order to calculate the net income per hectare of forest, we drew on the data from the Forest Management Plan of the Forest Management Unit Kranj (2012). The Forest Management Plan for the Kranj region states that the total income on a hectare of forest in government owned forests is €771. In forests that are owned by the local community or cooperatives a hectare of forest is worth €584. And in the privately owned forest the income on a hectare of forest is €1,038.

On the basis of different estimated incomes per hectare of forest, we could now determine land ownership. But because the data of each individual forest plot owner in Slovenia is not publicly available, it was necessary to rely on the official information from the Slovenian Forest Institute (2013) where it can be seen that more than 93% of forests in the upper part of the valley are privately owned. According to the official statistics (Table 2.1) it is thus clear that a hectare of forest land is worth €1,038 on average.

Table 2.1 – Calculation of income (Forest Management Plan for Kranj)

Revenue – value of timber	€2841 / ha
The cost of replanting, extraction and manipulation	€1617 / ha
The cost of cultivation and protection of forests	€122 / ha
The cost of road maintenance	€75 / ha
Maintenance of forest roads	€59 / ha
Maintenance of tracks	€15 / ha
Total cost	€1803 / ha
Income (revenue- expenses)	€1038 / ha

However, when calculating such a variable product as wood it is necessary to establish a parallel calculation for more accurate results. The data for the second calculation was taken from an independent research carried out at the Jemec estate in the upper part of the Selščica valley in the village of Davča (Jemec, 2010).

According to the second calculation on the Jemec estate the income per hectare of forest is €2,352 (Table 2.2). Taking into consideration both calculations it is then clear that the land owners would receive anything between €1,038 and €2,352 per hectare of forest by selling timber and wood products.

Table 2.2 – Calculation of income on Jemec Estate

Revenue – value of timber	€3549 / ha
Cost of cultivation and road construction	€353 / ha
The cost of logging and harvesting	€330 / ha
Cadastral income tax	€32 / ha
Maintenance of tracks	€132 / ha
Cost of management	€350 / ha
Other costs	€445 / ha
Total costs	€1197 / ha
Income (revenue–expenses)	€2352 / ha

Source: Jemec, 2010.

A positive conclusion can also be derived if we look at the key findings of a parallel research study that was conducted in Tuscany (Randelli, Romei, Tortora, & Mossello, 2011). Although this particular study depicts and analyses a broader variety of factors than just reforestation, what clearly transpires from its findings is the need for tourism development in the area identified as protected cultural landscape to be balanced and sustainable, and above all it must accord with a comprehensive set of socio–economic, cultural and geographic activities that maintain the landscape. Randelli and his colleagues also observed that the more a landscape preserves its traditional features, the greater its advantage with regards to future sustainable tourism development.

2.5. Conclusion

This chapter has primarily shown a direct economic value in forest reduction for the purpose of revealing the traditional cultural landscape of the upper part of the Selščica valley. To this end, approximately 7.7568 hectares of forest on 184 cadastral units of land in seven rural communities of the upper valley would have to be cut down.[7]

Taking into account that the average estate in the area measures 109 hectares (Jemec, 2010), the estimated number does not in fact represent a significant amount of forest for each individual land owner. By selling timber and wood products the forest owners in the upper part of the valley would collectively earn between €8,051 and €18,244.

However, it is important to also take into consideration alternative sources of income, primarily the auctioning of wood logs for various musical instruments. Based on the research, the fact that the majority of trees that would have to be cut down are rare alpine spruce (86%) and larch trees (10%) (Jelenc, 2007), and if according to the Forest and Forestry Portal of Slovenia (2014) approximately 5% of all the cut-down trees could be auctioned, it is estimated that the income gained from auction could be between €60,450 and €75,000 per hectare.[8]

It has been shown that cutting down the forest represents the biggest indirect economic benefit because it allows for the revitalization of the protected traditional cultural landscape that provides the foundation for sustainable tourism development in the future.

Overall findings thus present a key policy development tool that will not only bring positive economic effects but also an optimal starting point from which further management of cultural landscape as well as sustainable tourism development in the upper part of the Selščica valley can be pursued.

Last but not least, our research also represents a significant contribution to tourism and environmental studies while the methodology used is also applicable to numerous other cultural landscapes, provided accurate historic and cartographical data is followed for determining the economic benefits of each individual unit while maintaining the traditional landscape elements.

References

Environmental atlas of Slovenia (2013). Land cadastral units for the village of Sorica from 2013. Retrieved January 18, 2014, from http://gis.arso.gov.si/atlasokolja/profile.aspx?id=Atlas_Okolja_AXArso

Forest and Forestry Portal of Slovenia (2014). Auction of wood. Retrieved March 22, 2014, from http://www.gozd-les.com/upravljanje-gozdov/prodaja-lesa/licitacija-lesa

Forest Management Plan of the Forest Management Unit Kranj (2012). Forest in the region of Kranj. Retrieved January 5, 2014, from http://www.mko.gov.si/fileadmin/mko.gov.si/pageuplads/GGO/Kranj/03_KRANJ_2011-2020.pdf

Garrod, G., & Willis, K.G. (1999). *Economic valuation of the environment: methods and case studies*. Cheltenham: Edward Elgar.

Hanley, N., Barbier, E.B., & Barbier, E. (2009). *Pricing nature: cost-benefit analysis and environmental policy*. Northampton: Edward Elgar Publishing.

Jelenc, R. (2007). *Analiza upravičenosti žagarskega obrata v Selški dolini* (Analysis of entitlement of a sawmill plant in Selška valley). University of Ljubljana, Biotechnical Faculty, Department of Forestry and renewable forest resources.

Jemec, U. (2010). *Gozdnogospodarski načrt za Jemčevo gozdno posest* (Forest management plan for the Jemec estate). University of Ljubljana, Biotechnical Faculty, Department of Forestry and renewable forest resources.

Kobler, A. (2001). *Nove metode za obdelavo podatkov letalskega laserskega skenerja za monitoring gozdnih ekosistemov* (Acceptability of spontaneous afforestation with forest as a function of landscape) (Doctoral dissertation). University of Ljubljana, Faculty of Civil and Geodetic Engineering.

Markelj, M. (2009). *Tirolska arhitekturna in urbanistična dediščina v vaseh zgornje Selške doline* (Tyrol architecture heritage in the villages of the upper part of the Selščica valley). University of Primorska, Faculty of Humanities Koper.

—. (2011a). Arhitekturna raziskava – osnova za vzpostavitev več kot 800 let starih povezav (Architectural research – basis for the restoration of 800 years old connections). *Bank of Tourism Potentials in Slovenia*. Retrieved January 20, 2014, from https://www.btps.si/depositview.aspx?dpid=1340&lng=en

—. (2011b). *Vrednotenje turističnih resursov zgornjega dela Selške doline za izbrane turistične proizvode* (Evaluation of tourism resources of the

upper Selščica valley for selected tourism products). University of
Primorska, Faculty of Tourism Studies – Turistica.
—. (2012). Tirolska arhitekturna dediščina v vaseh zgornje Selške doline
(Tyrolean Architectural Heritage in the Villages of Zgornja Selška
Dolina). *Bulletin of Slovenian Ethnological Society*, 52(4), 58-65.
Ozdemiroglu, E., Tinch, R., Johns, H., Provins, A., Powell, J., &
Twiggers-Ross, C. (2006). *Valuing our natural environment – final
report*. (NR0103). London: Department for Environment, Food and
Rural Affairs. Retrieved February 21, 2014, from
http://earthmind.net/rivers/docs/ukdefra-eftec-valuing-our-natural-
environment.pdf
Pagiola, S., Ritter, K., & Bishop, J. (2004). *Assessing the economic value
of ecosystem conservation (Environmental department paper 101)*.
Washington: The World Bank. Retrieved February 22, 2014,
http://www.cbd.int/doc/pa/tools/Assessing%20the%20Economic%20V
alue%20of%20Ecosystem%20Conservation.pdf
Pearce, W.D., & Moran, D. in association with the Biodiversity program
of IUCN (1994). *The economic value of biodiversity*. New York:
Earthscan Publications.
Pearce, W.D., & Turner, K.R. (1990). *Economics of natural resources and
the environment*. Baltimore: Johns Hopkins University Press.
Pearce, W.D., & Turner, R.K. (1992). *Benefits, estimates and
environmental decision-making*. Paris: Organisation for Economic Co-
operation and Development.
Prewitt, R.A. (1949). *The economics of public recreation – an economic
survey of the Monetary Evaluation of Recreation in National Parks*.
Washington: National Park Services and Recreation Planning division.
Rajšp, V., & Srše, A. (1998). *Josephiniche Landesaufnahme 1763–1787*
(Slovenia on the military map 1763–1787). Ljubljana: Scientific and
Research Centre of the Slovenian Academy of Sciences and Arts and
the Archive of the Republic of Slovenia.
Randelli, F., Romei, P., Tortora M., & Mossello, M. (2011). *Rural tourism
driving regional development in Tuscany: the renaissance of the
countryside*. University of Florence, Department of Economics.
Register of Slovene cultural heritage. (2013). Franziscean land cadaster
map from the year 1825. Retrieved January 20, 2013, from
http://giskd6s.situla.org/giskd/
Ruzzier, M., Žujo, J., Marinšek, M., & Sosič, S. (2010). *Guidelines for the
economic valuation of ecosystem services in protected areas of nature*.
Ljubljana: Institute of the Republic of Slovenia for Nature
Conservation.

Slovenian Forest Institute (2013). Map of state owned forests in Slovenia for 2011. Retrieved January 17, 2014, from http://www.zgs.si/fileadmin/zgs/main/img/CE/gozdovi_SLO/Karte/Delez_zasebnih_gozdov.JPG

Slovenj Gradec wood auction (2014). Results of the 8th auction of wood in Slovenj Gradec. Retrieved May 15, 2014, from http://www.gozdles.com/novice/priprave-9-licitacijo-vrednejsega-lesa-2015

Tribe, J. (2005). *The economics of recreation, leisure and tourism.* Oxford: Elsevier Butterworth Heinemann.

Verbič, M., & Slabe, E.R. (2004). *Smernice za ekonomsko vrednotenje naravne in kulturne dediščine* (Guidelines for the economic valuation of natural and cultural heritage). Ljubljana: Institute for Economic Research.

Verbič, M., & Slabe, E.R. (2007). *Economic valuation of environmental values of the landscape development and protection area of Volčji Potok.* Ljubljana: Institute for Economic Research.

Notes

[1] Market price approach (MPA), Hedonistic pricing method (HPM), Travel cost method (TCM), Zone travel cost methods (ZTCM), Individual travel cost methods (ITCM), Random utility model (RUM), Damage cost avoid method (DCA), Loss of output approach (LOA), Choice modeling approach (CMA), Market approaches (Tribe, 2005), Contingent valuation method (CVM), Lost of output approach (LOA), Costs of illness methods (COI), Choice modeling approach (CMA), Total economic value methods (TEV), Cost Benefit Analysis (CBA) and Benefit transfer methods (BT).

[2] Some earlier studies also exist, dating back to the fifties where surveys that tried to determine the economic benefits of recreation in national parks were written (Prewitt, 1949).

[3] At the beginning of the 13th century the bishops from Freising (Germany) established a connection between two alpine valleys, the Pustartal valley (Hochpustertal or Alta Pusteria) in the Alto Adige/ Südtirol region of Italy and Selščica valley in the Gorenjska region in Slovenia. First written documents that go back as early as 1283, already depict the colonization of the upper part of the Selščica valley by the people from Tyrol, and this connection is notable for nearly 800 years (Markelj, 2011a).

[4] The oldest territorial map depicting individual land units and infrastructure for the present–day territory of Slovenia is the Josephine military map from 1763. Today the original documents are accessible in the National archive of Slovenia and a book series "Slovenia on the military map" (Rajšp & Srše, 1998), but the Franciscan land cadaster map that was made in the years from 1813 to 1827 is the

most accurate one while its measurements and estimations do not deviate greatly from today's measurements.

[5] The survey also examined the cultural features of the landscape in the time period between 1825 and 2013 (location of the road networks, the number of residential, commercial, administrative and religious buildings and religious monuments) but minimal changes were found, and their impact on the cultural landscape as a whole was found to be negligible.

[6] Zgornja and Spodnja Sorica are today the most urbanized village communities in the upper part of the Selščica valley thus the calculation has shown an increase in the non-forested cadastral units today in comparison to 1825.

[7] From the seven rural communities, 18 cadastral units would be cut down in the community Zgornja and Spodnja Sorica, 36 cadastral units in the community of Zgornje and Spodnje Danje, 21 cadastral units in Zabrdo community, 13 cadastral units in the community of Ravne and 96 cadastral units in Zali Log community.

[8] Above stated income has been derived from the calculation that the average price for one cubic meter of quality larch wood is between €243 and €749 and one cubic meter of spruce wood is between €199 and €930. The estimates have been taken from an auction in the town of Slovenj Gradec which took place on the 12th February 2014 (Slovenj Gradec wood auction, 2014).

CHAPTER THREE

SUSTAINABLE TOURISM: COMMUNITY–BASED TOURISM IN VIETNAM'S CENTRAL HIGHLANDS

THÁI HUỲNH ANH CHI

Abstract

Community-based tourism (CBT) is a recognized sustainable alternative to traditional forms of tourism development. Because CBT is seen as having the potential to alleviate poverty among indigenous people, CBT is expected to develop in Vietnam's Central Highlands – a mountainous area which is home to a variety of ethnic minorities. However, given the specific socio-economic and ecological conditions in this area, some risks threaten CBT's sustainability when it is targeted towards poverty alleviation. This chapter examines the impact of CBT in this context and attempts to identify the best ways to utilize CBT in Vietnam's Central Highlands. **Keywords:** community-based tourism, poverty alleviation, sustainable development, Vietnam.

3.1. Introduction

The Central Highlands, a mountainous area on the western flank of the Annamite Mountains, form a high plateau along Vietnam's western borders with Cambodia and Laos. This area is home to a large population of indigenous ethnic groups. In the past, these groups comprised the majority of the population and claimed ownership of the area's vast swaths of unclaimed land. Until 1975, these indigenous groups accounted for 69.7% of the population. Only a relatively small group of ethnic Vietnamese, the so-called Kinh people, had settled in this region at the beginning of colonial times (United States Agency for International Development, 2008).

However, this ratio dramatically reversed after the Vietnam War, when the Vietnamese government implemented a series of institutional and policy reforms in this area (Ha & Shively, 2008; United States Agency for International Development, 2008). One of the biggest plans involved the claiming of agricultural land and resettling the Kinh people to the Highlands (Dang Thanh Ha, 2001; Pam McElwee, 2001). Thus, the indigenous people suddenly became the minorities on their own land, comprising only 27% of the population (General Statistics Office, 2009). Through such policy reforms, this area has achieved success via diverse and high output agricultural production (Espaldon et al., 2004). However, the output from land occupied by the indigenous people lags seriously behind (Writnet, 2006). This trend has aroused concern and a desire among locals and scholars to find a solution that will enable the indigenous people to reduce their poverty and relieve the imbalance between their society and that of the Kinh.

Due to tourism's potential to induce macro-economic growth in less highly developed countries, a variety of international institutions have implemented various programs to promote tourism as an economic development tool. CBT emerges from this trend. The term "community-based tourism" refers to a form of tourism in which the local community maintains substantial control. CBT not only helps local villagers control the impact of tourism, but also generates additional income and diversifies the local economy (Tuffin, 2005). A number of CBT projects have been carried out in different communities in developing countries. In Vietnam, the government has partnered with international institutions and NGOs in recent decades to launch a range of projects promoting CBT for poverty alleviation. Following the success of some pilot projects in the Northern Highlands, CBT is expected to achieve the same purpose of poverty alleviation in the Central Highlands.

However, it would be missing the point to ignore the deeper implications of CBT: the assumption that this kind of tourism reduces poverty but has no other impact on the people involved in it is short-sighted and does not take the surrounding socio-cultural or ecological context into consideration. Ideally, CBT requires redefinition, reinterpretation, and translation every time new actors are involved in the process (Zapata, Hall, Lindo, & Vanderschaeghe, 2011). Given the specific conditions in Vietnam's Central Highlands, some skepticism about CBT's ability to alleviate indigenous poverty on a large scale seems natural. This paper therefore examines CBT in this context and proposes ways in which the parties involved can implement CBT in the region. It also considers how consistently and intensively CBT should be developed.

3.2. Literature Review

Since the 1980s, several alternative forms and strategies of tourism have been introduced: soft/low impact, green/eco/cultural/responsible forms of tourism, and community-based approaches (Pimrawee, 2005). The concept of CBT first emerged in the work of Murphy (1985) as a response to the negative impact of the international mass tourism development model. CBT has become widely recognized as an example of a sustainable development approach, and is considered a form of bottom-up management (Pimrawee, 2005). The APEC tourism working group defines CBT as a community development tool. CBT can help communities by generating income, diversifying the local economy, preserving cultural heritage, conserving the environment, and providing educational opportunities. CBT does not only come to be seen as a poverty reduction tool (Hamzah & Khalifah, 2009), it is also said to bring "hope" to communities in need, and especially to those in the developing world.

Since CBT is considered a development tool (Hamzah & Khalifah, 2009), almost all studies to date have recognized CBT as an alternative that can remedy the adverse effects of conventional tourism. It has perhaps been too readily believed that poverty will be alleviated when the poorest sections of a nation are involved in CBT. This assumption reveals the superficiality of placing trust in CBT as an unquestionable poverty "cure all". Though CBT aims to maximize benefits for the local community and limit the potential negative impact of tourism, can a balance between conservation and economic concerns be achieved (Godde, 1998)? Ayres criticizes CBT, noting that "there is no guarantee that the benefits of tourism will trickle down to the poorest groups, nor does tourism necessarily reduce inequalities" (Ayres, 2000). In addition, since CBT offers tourists the chance to closely interact with the community, it might trigger conflicts apart from those associated with unequally-shared profits (which CBT attempts to solve), by threatening a community's cultural identity and social stability. Moreover, focusing on the economic goal of poverty reduction alone forces tourism activities to expand toward a more mainstream level. Halim has highlighted that "tourism for poverty alleviation should be expanded and applicable in mainstream (mass) tourism" (Halim, 2010). Vulnerable local groups that depend heavily on tourism for economic survival may then be at risk for losing business. CBT also has its own entrenched threats, like any form of tourism. While CBT has the potential to bring economic, ecological, and socio–cultural benefits, it contains several inherent dilemmas that must be recognized (Godde, 1998).

As Tosun (2000, p.613) states, "the concept of community tourism has been developed and refined in the context of developed countries in search of sustainable approaches to tourism development. However, the applicability of such a concept to developing countries seems to not have been considered in detail". Furthermore, according to Baum, even well–intentioned aspirations for development can go wrong when the approach remains superficial and does not fully recognize the specific characteristics of the community's concern   (Baum, 1996). Likewise, Zapata also discusses the process of adapting CBT projects to their local contexts (Zapata *et al.*, 2011). Poorly implemented CBT projects can create adverse results. Therefore, it is essential to consider the context of each community and carefully assess CBT's potential before implementing it.

3.3. Methodology

So far, most of the research on CBT has been implemented under two approaches. Initial studies apply statistical techniques to evaluate the effects of CBT and measure the attitudes of stakeholders. Other studies have developed and tested theories. This study was conducted during the very early stages of CBT development in the Central Highlands. The empirical on-site studies enable an understanding of communities' circumstances. The results also contribute to CBT theory when answering the question of whether or not CBT is an ideal (or even realistic) approach, while also serving as a first step for forthcoming CBT projects in the Central Highlands.

Although qualitative methodology is predominant, this research uses a mixed method approach. The data was collected throughout the observation and participation periods. In addition, secondary data played an important role when presenting fundamental information about the poverty status and socio-economic conditions of the indigenous people in the Central Highlands. The necessary data was collected from Vietnam's General Statistics Office (GSO) and other local offices. The combination of this data and the survey data allows for a rigorous analysis of the various phases of CBT's development in the Central Highlands.

As mentioned above, since this research was conducted in an area where CBT is at a very early stage, and the complete picture of CBT activities in this area has not yet been formed, we employ the scenario method to estimate possible outcomes. This tool is valuable for such studies because the scenario method is one way of foreseeing the future and helps to clarify uncertainties (Pimrawee, 2005). Given the outcome of some CBT projects operating in similar areas, and the overall economic situation in the Central Highlands, this study analyzes the possible output of CBT development as a poverty alleviation tool in this area. Next, both the internal and external factors, and both negative and positive sides of applying CBT, are assessed, via a process called "SWOT analysis". The acronym SWOT stands for strengths, weaknesses, opportunities, and threats (Goranczewski & Puciato, 2010). Since tourism development is influenced by multiple factors, this method is employed to construct an overall evaluation of CBT in this context.

3.4. Results

The results point out both the external (opportunities and threats) and internal (strengths and weaknesses) factors of tourism development. Sustainable tourism is based on three principle pillars: social justice, economic development, and environmental integrity (International Labour Organization, 2011). The opportunities, threats, strengths, and weaknesses are analyzed in regard to these three pillars, analyses which will then provide an overview before applying CBT as an alleviation tool in the Vietnam Central Highlands.

3.4.1. Strengths and opportunities

Based on the region's ideal combination of natural resources and unique cultural value, tourism can likely blossom in this area if it is invested in and promoted as a mass-trend. The advantages of developing CBT in Vietnam's Central Highlands have both internal and external dimensions.

Tourism potential in the Central Highlands

The Central Highlands offer tourists an itinerary which diverges from the standard routes in Vietnam. The Central Highlands might not be as outstanding as the northern mountains in terms of scenic beauty, but they convey a distinct purity and charm. The Central Highlands have long had the richest and most densely forested areas in Vietnam; forest covered 54.6% of the region in 2006, although it had unfortunately been reduced to 52.4% by 2014. The Central Highlands are also home to some of the most prominent and most endangered species in Vietnam and Southeast Asia. Though most of the Highlands have been converted to plantations, the primary forests are still preserved and sustain incredibly diverse wildlife, including elephants, bears, and gibbons. This area now contains five national parks, namely Chư Mom Ray (Kon Tum), Kon Ka Kinh (Gia

Lai), Yok Đôn, Chư Yang Sin (DakLak), and Bi doup Núi Bà (Lam
Dong). The forest is considered one of the most significant sources of
capital in the area. The Central Highlands stretch across a series of
contiguous plateaus, a topography which creates breathtaking views of
mountainous landscapes and frequently draws tourists. The Central
Highlands are also home to a system of spectacular waterfalls, due to the
region's distinctive short, steep rivers.

In addition, the colourful cultural identities present in the Central
Highlands and the distinct cultural value of indigenous groups in particular
are considered the most precious asset and significant source of potential
capital for developing CBT. Even though they now account for only one
third of the population in the Central Highlands, the indigenous people
still shape the charm and mystery of this area with their cultural identity.
Their cultural value, which has been accumulated over generations and
embedded in their daily lives in the form of customs and beliefs, is also a
major source of attraction for this area. Some of their beliefs and customs,
such as festivals and artistic performances, traditional architecture,
handicrafts, their colourful traditional dress, and traditional cuisine can be
converted into tourism products. Thus, the nature, culture, history, and
rural life which are inherent in the Central Highlands can be considered
positive factors from which CBT can be developed.

Opportunities for developing CBT in Vietnam's Central Highlands

The Central Highlands have the advantage of sharing a border with
southern Laos and north-eastern Cambodia. Thanks to the facilitation of
the pre-existing economic infrastructure and the advantages of cross-
border traffic, this area grants easy access to the neighbouring countries.
Transnational tourism and a combination of destinations are therefore
possible. Even though the market share still presents a significant
deviation between domestic and foreign tourists, this area has recently
welcomed more foreign tourists than it did in previous years: The number
of foreign tourists travelling to the Central Highlands increased from
81,376 arrivals in 2000 to 235,850 arrivals in 2010. Besides the traditional
market from Western countries, South Asia has been evaluated as a
dynamic potential market for tourism; this is thus an opportunity for the
development of tourism in the Central Highlands.

3.4.2. Weaknesses and threats of developing CBT

Though the Central Highlands have a distinct tourism potential that can be
utilized by the indigenous people to alleviate their poverty, clarification on

some issues must be encouraged before applying tourism as a mainstream activity in this area.

Poverty status and heavy dependence on agriculture

Although Vietnam's economy has gradually progressed over the past 30 years, there is evidence that ethnic minorities continue to face many hardships and minority communities still experience high rates of poverty (Figure 3.1). Within the general trend of high levels of poverty among ethnic minorities, the minorities of the Central Highlands have stood out for many years as being some of the worst off. In 1998, 91% of the Central Highlands' minority population lived in poverty, compared to 73% of minorities in the Northern uplands (Writnet, 2006). This rate fell to 51.8% in 2002 and 24.1% in 2008, while corresponding poverty rates for the whole country were 28.9% and 14.5%, respectively (General Statistic Office, 2008). Additionally, the poverty rates mentioned here are only defined in terms of income; these figures cannot describe the exact status of poverty in these areas because the indigenous people also rely on natural forest products for food, fodder, medicine, and construction materials (D.Sunderlin & Ba, 2005), and such aspects of their livelihoods are inevitably excluded from statistics. However, it is obvious that indigenous people in the Central Highlands are living below the standards of other regions.

In the past, indigenous people had depended heavily on agriculture and engaged in shifting cultivation for their living. Recently, the indigenous people's traditional system of agricultural production has changed due to the Vietnamese government restricting shifting cultivation, simultaneously encouraging sedentary agriculture and increased production of cash crops. Agriculture now remains a pillar in the indigenous people's lives. However, after the process of collectivization and subsequent decollectivization, the indigenous people do not regain the same amount of land they had donated. Instead, only a fraction of their former lands are returned to them (United States Agency for International Development, 2008). At present, on smaller plots of land and lacking knowledge of intensive agriculture, the indigenous people cannot be as productive as the Kinh. Some of them still keep their less effective traditional crops, 87% of indigenous people not cultivating industrial crops (The World Bank, 2009).

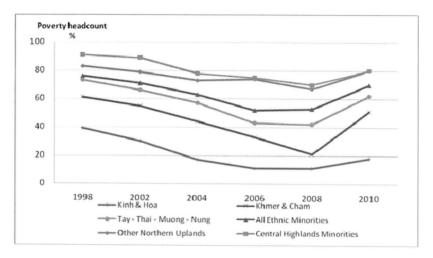

Figure 3.1 - Poverty rates among different ethnic groups in Vietnam, 1998 – 2010
Source: Vietnam Households Living Standard Survey, General Statistic Office and
World Bank.

Another major source of income among indigenous people is forestry. At
present, however, indigenous people benefit much less from forestry than
they did before. As in other Southeast Asian countries, the lion's share of
timber wealth goes to the government's treasury and private entrepreneurs.
The ethnic minorities have been excluded from direct access to timber
(D.Sunderlin & Ba, 2005). Also, trade was once a dominant system of
interaction between the indigenous people of this area and outsiders or
lowlanders, such as the Kinh. The indigenous people often exchanged
forest products, traditional instruments, and handicrafts for salt and food
from the lowlands (Pamela McElwee, 2008). Yet, although many of
today's ethnic minorities participate in trade, they have largely been
excluded by middlemen from managing their own trade and have been
unable to increase their share of market prices or value-added goods,
instead selling mostly raw, unprocessed products at low prices (The World
Bank, 2009).

It can be said that the economic activities of indigenous people have
been based on the land and forests for centuries. According to a statistic
from 2010, agriculture accounted for 49.1% of the Central Highlands'
income, whereas the industrial sector accounted for 21.8 % and services
(mainly tourism) contributed 29.1%.

The fragile environment and sensitive culture of this mountainous area

First and foremost, the fragility of the mountain ecosystems, which lies in their biological and cultural characteristics, needs to be considered. To make matters worse, while these systems are fragile and prone to damage, their restoration process is very slow and in some cases they do not recuperate themselves (Batta, 2000). Therefore, any form of mass-production poses a constant threat to the ecosystem. Conversation is one of the first targets for any development project in a mountainous area, and so far, tourism in this area has not yet become mainstream or resulted in detrimental consequences to the environment. However, a clear lesson can be learned from the agricultural sector in this area. After the Vietnam War, the Vietnamese government introduced some economic policies, institutions, and opportunities for market access that encouraged intensive agriculture and led to a large-scale transformation of forestland into cropland. In the nearly four decades since this project was carried out, this area has become highly successful in cash crop cultivation, which has helped Vietnam become the second highest coffee-exporter in the world. However, the rapid expansion and intensification of agricultural production on the fragile marginal land, driven in part by an expanding population, has also placed high pressure on natural resources and caused highly negative consequences in the uplands. High rates of forest degradation and high soil erosion and a decreased watershed threaten agricultural sustainability (Dang Thanh Ha, 2001).

In addition, despite their long history of planting diverse subsistence crops, the indigenous people have not benefitted from this practice. Recently, the national and local government have expended a great deal of effort to overcome the negative environmental and social consequences of intensive agricultural development (Dang Thanh Ha, 2001). Given the current situation of agricultural development in the Central Highlands, great care must be taken to avoid further exploiting natural resources for the purpose of tourism.

Turning back to tourism itself, recreation per se is largely non-consumptive compared to agriculture, mining, or forestry (Batta, 2000). However, when more and more people visit the mountains, tourism also results in some adverse effects on areas that previously had a low population density. In addition, the more tourists that appear, the more infrastructure and tourism facilities are built up that could disturb the mountains' ecosystem. Therefore, it is important to control the rhythm and flow of tourism in mountainous areas, and the concept of carrying capacity must be considered carefully. Due to the fragility of uplands, an excess capacity is likely to promote varying levels of damage. Moreover, tourism products in the Central Highlands depend heavily on the natural landscape and environment, such that a massive influx of tourists can threaten environmental resources. If this occurs, the symbiotic relationship between tourism and the environment cannot be maintained and the region will not even be able to satisfy local needs, much less tourist demands.

Another fragile aspect in mountainous areas is the sensitive culture of the indigenous people. The distinctive culture in the Central Highlands is derived from the indigenous people, who have long lived on and owned the land. So far, they have preserved their customs, beliefs, and group institutions, which pique the curiosity of both scholars and tourists. However, the indigenous people are also characterized by their poverty, unemployment, and illiteracy. Their culture is so sensitive that USAID has assessed them as one of the most vulnerable groups in the Central Highlands (United States Agency for International Development, 2008). This vulnerability, therefore, places some barriers to developing mass tourism in the area. CBT in particular, which allows tourists to penetrate deeply into the personal lives of local people, can generate both social and cultural impact. In addition, when CBT aims to empower the indigenous people by granting them sufficient ownership to control and develop tourism, additional issues may emerge. The indigenous people have previously based their income heavily on agriculture and lack the knowledge, skills, and experience necessary to run service industries such as tourism. Some inappropriate practices may lead to the exploitation of resources in favor of short-term gains.

Another equally important problem is ongoing local unrest related to land rights and religious freedom (McElwee, 2001; Writnet, 2006). When researching the factors responsible for environmental degradation in mountainous areas, Batta (2000) indicates that the prevailing patterns of inequitable land ownership and population growth in many mountainous developing countries have led to a scarcity of arable land which contributes to an increased strain on subsistence communities. This scenario is exactly the case for the Central Highlands. The circumstances in the Central Highlands necessitate careful consideration of these potential dangers before tourism, even in the case of CBT, should be increased to an intensive level. Moreover, from a sustainability view, it is recommended that when promoting cultural value and exposing it to tourists, limitations need to be put into place to prevent the culture itself from becoming a commodity.

For cultural identities as distinctive as those in the Central Highlands in particular, excess exposure to mass-tourism services may lead to socio-economic risks, as has been demonstrated in Sapa, the site of one of

Vietnam's CBT pilots. Located in northern Vietnam, Sapa is famous for its spectacular landscape and colorful culture and is appealing to both local and international tourists. While income can be increased easily and quickly with the implementation of tourist activities, the local people – as was the case in Sapa – may be tempted to exploit their cultural value beyond a reasonable level by transferring it into both planned and spontaneous tourist products. Consequently, this practice creates cultural instability within a society. The younger men may lose interest in their traditional farming activities and the younger women may turn to offering unhealthy or inappropriate services. Children may abandon school in order to earn money by working for street vendors. Thus the immediate appeal of profit promotes the loss of cultural richness and potentially of self-esteem. This cycle ultimately leads to another more immaterial poverty, even though the average income may have increased with the accelerated economic growth rate.

Threats of developing CBT as a poverty alleviation tool

Last but not least, some external factors also threaten sustainable tourism in the Central Highlands, particularly when CBT is implemented on a mass level that forces indigenous people to rely on this economic activity. The tourism sector is generally assumed to be significantly affected by the market. Upheavals in international financial markets can adversely affect both international and domestic tourism in Vietnam. As a vulnerable group, the ethnic minorities in the Central Highlands should not depend heavily on tourism for economic survival; otherwise, they might face greater risk during times of market fluctuation, and ultimately be left with greater unrest and more burdens than they have faced previously. Also, the competitiveness of other, more well-known neighboring destinations inhibits the local community from gaining an entirely stable livelihood from tourism.

In addition, the climate in the Central Highlands is characterized by two very distinct seasons: dry and wet. Thus the landscape always changes tremendously between the seasons, and tourist activities in this area are limited by a very high degree of seasonality. During the wet season, from May to November, the roads are regularly washed out, yet the region is likely to be more beautiful when the landscape is fresh and alive with tumbling rivers, waterfalls, and mist. During the dry season, on the other hand humidity sharply decreases: the rivers drain, and the scenery appears drab. Seasonality thus poses an additional problem for tourism development in the Central Highlands, so it is difficult to ensure a continuous flow of income from tourism for the local people.

From the above discussion, it becomes apparent that maintaining sustainable CBT development in the Central Highlands is a real challenge. When applying CBT as a poverty alleviation tool and thus focusing heavily on economic purposes alone, an environment and culture as fragile as that of the Central Highlands might be at risk of damage. Thus an appropriate balance which takes ecological, economic, and socio-cultural elements into account must be integrated into CBT activities before it can be safely implemented in an area like the Central Highlands.

3.5. Conclusion

The Central Highlands have potential, both in their natural resources and cultural value, to form a distinctive tourism product. Tourism can bring improvements to the lives of local people by increasing their income. However, some underlying threats to sustainable development, derived from both internal and external conditions, may push communities into an even harsher life if tourism becomes mainstream and local people depend too heavily on it. Community-based tourism in mountainous areas like the Central Highlands should not be considered an enterprise that solves everything, and especially cannot be seen as an effective poverty alleviation tool. Rather, it should be seen as a supplemental means of income, when used in combination with other sustainable sources of livelihood (Godde, 1998). By acknowledging that growth alone will not address persistent poverty in mountainous regions, it is necessary to integrate and determine the place for tourism in the local community's economy.

In the case of Vietnam's Central Highlands, it is essential to bear in mind that agriculture and forestry have formed the basis of the traditional economy, and that these activities should remain the primary economic sectors in the region. These activities contribute the most to poverty alleviation, while offering the greatest opportunities for achieving impact on a meaningful scale. They also provide the most reliable source of employment for ethnic minority households. Therefore, the challenge for CBT development lies in how to integrate it into the pre-existing economy. Strategies to reduce poverty in the Central Highlands should be small-scale, applicable to the long-term, and both culturally and environmentally sustainable. When developing tourism in mountainous areas such as the Central Highlands, the objective of tourism practices must be focused toward human and environmental values, rather than concentrating solely on economic gain.

References

Ayres, R. (2002). Cultural tourism in small-island states: Contradictions and ambiguities. In Y. Apostolopoulos, & D.J. Gayle (eds.). *Island tourism and sustainable development: Caribbean, Pacific and Mediterranean experiences* (pp.145-160). Westport, CT: Praeger Publishers.

Baum, T. (1996). Tourism and the host community: A cautionary tale. *Tourism Management, 17*(2), 149–150.

D.Sunderlin, W., & Ba, H.T. (2005). *Poverty alleviation and forests in Vietnam* (p. 73). Indonesia: Center for International Forest Research, Bogor, Indonesia.

Dang Thanh Ha, M.V.O.E. (2001). Balancing economic and environmental concerns in the Uplands of Vietnam: A continuing challenge. *SANREM CRSP Research Scientific Synthesis Conference.* Athens, GA.

Espaldon, D.M.V.O., Phuoc, P.H.D., Thuy, N.N., Du, L. Van, Hung, P.T., Thong, L.Q., ... Ha, D.T. (2004). Challenges on sustainable agriculture and natural resource management in Vietnam uplands: A case study. SEAMEO SEARCA.

General Statistics Office (2009). *The 2009 Vietnam population and housing Census.* (Central population and housing census steering committee, Ed.). Ha Noi.

Godde, P. (1998). *Community-based mountain tourism: Practices for linking conservation with enterprise* (P. Godde, Ed.). Mountain Forum.

Goranczewski, B., & Puciato, D. (2010). SWOT analysis in the formulation of tourism development strategies for destinations. *Tourism.* 20(2), 45-54.

Ha, D.T., & Shively, G. (2008). Coffee boom, coffee bust and smallholder response in Vietnam's Central Highlands. *Review of Development Economics, 12*(2), 312–326.

Halim, N.A. (2010). M*ainstreaming tourism for rural poverty alleviation using value chain analysis: A case in Penarik, Terengganu, Malaysia.* Workshop on Tourism Development and Poverty Reduction in Sydney, Australia.

Hamzah, A., & Khalifah, Z. (2009). *Handbook on community-based tourism: "How to develop and sustain CBT."* Apec tourism working group. Retrieved from http://scholar.google.com/scholar?hl=en&btnG=Search&q=intitle:Han dbook+on+Community+Based+Tourism+"How+to+Develop+and+Sus tain+CBT"#0

International Labour Organization (2011). *Toolkit on poverty reduction through Tourism in rural areas.*

McElwee, P. (2001). Coffee, Christianity and conflict: An update on the Central Highlands of Vietnam. *Mekong Update & Dialogue, 4*(3), 8.

—. (2008). "Blood Relatives" or Uneasy Neighbors? Kinh Migrant and ethnic minority interactions in the Trường Sơn Mountains. *Journal of Vietnamese Studies, 3*(3), 81–116.

Pimrawee, R. (2005). *Community-based tourism: Perspectives and future.* James Cook.

The World Bank (2009). *Country social analysis ethnicity and development in Vietnam.*

Tosun, C. (2000). Limits to community participation in the tourism development process in developing countries. *Tourism Management, 21*, 613–633.

Tuffin, B. (2005). Community-based tourism in the Lao PDR: An overview. NAFRI; NAFES; NUOL. Retrieved from http://scholar.google.com/scholar?hl=en&btnG=Search&q=intitle:Community-Based+Tourism+in+the+Lao+PDR+:+An+Overview#1

United States Agency for International Development (2008). Vietnam Central Highlands needs assessment. USAID.

Writnet. (2006). Vietnam: Situation of indigenous minority groups in the Central Highlands. WRITENET Independent analysis.

Zapata, M.J., Hall, C.M., Lindo, P., & Vanderschaeghe, M. (2011). Can community-based tourism contribute to development and poverty alleviation? Lessons from Nicaragua. *Current Issues in Tourism, 14*(8), 725–749.

Chapter Four

Salient Stakeholder Identification for Forestry–Based Eco–Tourism Management

Hin Wai Yip, Abdullah Mohd, Wan Razali W.M., Manohar M. and Awang Noor A.G.

Abstract

Stakeholder participation in eco–tourism is important for destination sustainability. The process involves stakeholder identification, which assists destination managers in identifying the salient stakeholders. The objective of this chapter is to assess the stakeholder identification process and to determine the causal factors from the perspective of managers. A statistically sound model is presented to explain some preliminary ideas about how these factors and approaches to improvement would be linked to the salient stakeholders' features. The findings show that the strengthening of human capital is necessary in order to improve managers' skills in identifying salient stakeholders. **Keywords:** salient stakeholder, strategic approach, eco–tourism, Peninsular Malaysia.

4.1. Introduction

Stakeholder involvement has to take place in the initial stage of the eco–tourism development process. It is important for the sustainable use of tourism destinations. The idea is that many entities, either individuals or organizations, might claim to have a stake in or to be impacted by tourism development. These entities are able to influence the development process if they are able to strengthen their claims and to get them recognized and accepted by the administrative authorities in the area. Consequently, by involving the most relevant stakeholders in the planning process, it is vital for organisations to adhere to the sustainable development concept (Currie, Seaton, & Wesley, 2009). Stakeholder management is widely used by contemporary organizations, but some managers tend to keep a list of stakeholders only for their own or for their agency's operational purposes. This practice may not go as planned if an organization needs to involve those other than the individuals or parties of interests traditionally known to them. Therefore, managers need to update and enlarge their stakeholder pool to cover and engage those who had not previously been considered to be their stakeholders (Freeman, 1984).

In Malaysia, Forestry Departments offer and manage various forest–based recreational areas that have the potential to be further re–developed into eco–tourism destinations. However, due to the department's lengthy association with forest management and services, eco–tourism occurring in a forested setting was, until recently, given relatively little attention. When ecotourism, along with other supporting services, is stressed by the government, it encourages the department to look again at the distribution of resources in fulfilling such changes. In examining such developments, the department has no choice but to consider adopting the corporate approach in their operations, which includes managing their stakeholders. Thus, incorporating strategic approaches such as the stakeholder identification procedure could assist forest managers to determine their salient stakeholders (Simpson, 2001). This process involves identifying which groups of individuals or organizations are to be considered as their partners in strategic planning for forestry–based eco–tourism. Those making claims not considered by managers to be stakeholders are stake–seekers, with whom managers may need to engage from time to time.

4.2. Literature Review

In recent years, more people are going on retreats to recreational forests during their holidays to pursue healthy living. In conjunction with this increasing demand, forest recreation and eco–tourism activities are on the rise, especially in the permanent reserve forests (PRFs) close to urban centers. These are different from national parks, which are designated for conservation and recreation, in that certain PRFs offer services to the public. Moreover, these protected areas are managed by a range of public agencies with different goals. PRFs are mainly managed for forest resources extraction and forest-based environmental services. According to the Malaysian National Forestry Act 1984, of a total 12 types of functional forests, only two are meant for recreation and eco–tourism activities, Amenity Forest and State Park Forest.

In addition, as highlighted by Hurst (1990), the federal authority has limited executive power in state forestry matters, because the Malaysian Federal Constitution clearly states that forest matters are under the state's jurisdiction. As such, the federal authority's role is limited to providing the forest policy and a uniform forestry law to state governments (except for Sabah and Sarawak). In contrast, the implementation is highly dependent on each state authority and individual state's land use policy. Although there is a Forestry Department Headquarter in Peninsular Malaysia, forest management is a highly decentralized activity (Mohd & Yaman, 2001). The Forestry Department Headquarter, which acts on behalf of the federal government, only provides technical advice for the states in Peninsular Malaysia. Current forest management practices are based on the policy collectively agreed upon by state governments. Due to the complexity of forest governance and institutional issues, the present chapter will focus only on forest departments in Peninsular Malaysia.

Forest management is based upon the concept of Sustainable Forest Management (SFM) practices. The foundation for this implementation is the execution of National Forestry Policy in 1978, a policy strengthened as a result of its amendment in 1992 (Yasmi, Broadhead, Enters, & Genge, 2010). In this policy, the aim of SFM was defined as "to manage the forest in accordance with the principles of sustainable yield management for the maximization of social, economic and environmental benefits to the nation." Management practices were required to be socially equitable, economically viable, and environmentally acceptable, in line with the three pillars of sustainable development. Similarly, in stressing sustainability, eco–tourism development could also be managed as part of existing SFM practices. Nevertheless, when dealing with eco–tourism issues, the Forestry Department needs to engage with more stakeholders. They have to deal with those who are interested in forest management, as well as those who are interested in eco–tourism management.

4.2.1. Forestry–based eco–tourism and stakeholders

Developing eco–tourism in PRFs is part of the Malaysian national economic transformation program. Thus, it could attract a greater number of parties interested in taking advantage of it for their own benefit. As custodians for forest security, Forestry Departments need to take proactive steps to leverage various stakeholders, as this integrated task is neither the sole responsibility of these departments nor the exclusive responsibility of other interested parties. Forestry Departments need to work closely with these organizations. The challenge for forest managers is to find an effective and economically viable way of identifying the right partners. A strategic approach should be used in defining and identifying the right stakeholders (Yip, Abdullah, Wan Razali, Manohar, & Awang Noor, 2012).

In most cases, stakeholders are determined by the legitimacy of an organization from the perspective of managers, and not based on the external organization's interest in the issue. There is existing guidance for Forestry Departments in the stakeholder identification process. Malaysia applies Malaysian Criteria and Indicators (MC&I) for the Forest Management Certification in forest management, and stakeholder issues are handled in such a way as to ensure PRFs are sustainably managed, in line with the international standard. However, it should be noted that this standard focuses mainly on managing the forests for sufficient timber resources and the effectiveness of its environmental services. Social usage, which includes recreation and tourism, is one of many social functions of PRFs. Nonetheless, the contributions of environmental services and timber resources are usually more visible. Unlike their counterparts in national parks that focus on conservation, forest managers need to seek a balance between forest production, environmental services, and tourism activities. Managers might misinterpret or overlook other issues that are more pertinent when managing these forest reserves. Based on such a narrow approach, passive or latent stakeholders who do not project their opinions, and other potential but ignorant entities are likely to be overlooked by managers. These parties may not be considered to have a stake, and are likely to be left out of the consultation process.

Additionally, stakeholders are normally identified according to the needs of industries (Krick, Forstater, Monaghan, & Sillanpää, 2005). In forestry, stakeholders are those who are closer to the forest environment and wood–based industries, including the indigenous people (Colfer, 2005). However, the focal point shifted when eco–tourism came under the jurisdiction of forest management practices. Nevertheless, the eco–tourism industry has a different view on stakeholders, because they identify stakeholders from their own perspective. They are more concerned with the sustainability of the tourism industry, which includes various levels of community members: environmental, social, and community NGOs, natural resource, planning, and government officials, hotel owners, tour operators, guides, transportation providers, and representatives from other related services in the private sector (Sinha, 2006). This might result in the neglect of certain issues voiced by one concerned group but considered as less important by the other. Conflicts of interests can occur if concerns and interests are not appropriately addressed and resolved (Primmer & Kyllönen, 2006). This might have repercussions, for instance stake–seekers trying to gain attention by various means, such as gathering support from the public through social movements (King, 2008; Zietsma & Winn, 2008).

Even though guidelines for eco–tourism stakeholder identification are available for protected areas, priorities differ between forest managers and tourism players (Lindberg, Furze, Staff, & Black, 1997). Both players might share a similar interest in conserving the natural environment but disagree on the extent of tourism development that would jeopardize conservation efforts. Furthermore, organizations that claim to have a stake might not be viewed as stakeholders by managers. However, this view is only partially true, at least from the operational planning perspective (Fassin, 2009). The ignorance of certain groups could lead to some issues being overlooked. These disregarded issues might be highlighted later by stake-seekers (Lawrence, Wickins, & Philips, 1997). After that, conflicts of interest might follow if the issue is not properly handled. Therefore, to avoid such situations, managers have to ensure that every opinion is heard, and this relies on the implementation of a comprehensive stakeholder identification process. In such situations, forest departments need to get a comprehensive view on those who should be involved in the development, and they need to clearly identify which organizations should be engaged. For this reason, the definition of stakeholders should be reassessed to ensure various groups are included in the consultation process, especially those that could act as game–changers (Winn, 2001).

4.2.2. Salient stakeholders for eco–tourism

Engaging with salient stakeholders as early as possible would increase the possibility of eco–tourism development moving along the right track. In the corporate sector, managers need to compete in a dynamic environment and to avoid making the wrong decision. A small misjudgment would incur high costs to the management and delay progress. Similarly, the forestry departments of Malaysia are facing challenging times ahead, with more stakeholders recognizing their stakes and claiming them, particularly in eco–tourism development through PRFs.

Since 2010, the Performance Management and Delivery Unit (PEMANDU), a unit under the Prime Minister's Department, has identified the tourism industry as one of the National Key Economic Areas (NKEAs) in the Malaysian Economic Transformation Program (ETP).

This industry will be one of the key areas used as a driver for economic generation of the country in the new era. Under this program, eco–tourism has been identified as one of the components of tourism that is becoming a focal point for further development (PEMANDU, 2010). Thus, the forest custodians have to manage these claims and secure forest sustainability, in line with their forestry policy. Additionally, the Malaysian government has adopted a slogan, "People First, Performance Now" (*Rakyat didahulukan, Pencapaian Diutamakan*), which stresses the performance driven and effective management of public agencies while serving the people. Therefore, to achieve this objective, departments need to integrate corporate approaches into public administration by managing their stakeholders more effectively and catering for their needs without jeopardizing their authority upon PRFs.

Importantly, a rightful identification of stakeholders from a pool of various organizations with different vested interests is a skill that forest managers need to acquire. During the initial phase, the interested groups may share a common and amicable position on forestry and eco–tourism. At this juncture, different groups have tended to have different hidden agendas or vested interests that are then brought forward. The problem arises since most forest managers identify salient stakeholders mainly relying on conventional approaches. The identification method used is based on the parties' physical proximity to resources. This situation prevents stakeholders who are more salient than others being identified, especially during the planning stage.

In response, Mitchell, Agle and Wood (1997) have suggested a typology framework of stakeholders. This framework segregates the interest organizations/agencies according to their influence on management decision, by using the attributes of power, legitimacy, and urgency. Additionally, the difference between an operational and strategic approach in identifying stakeholders depends greatly on how the word "legitimacy" is defined. The strategic approach understands legitimacy as the appropriateness of including an organization/agency in the process, as opposed to the more widely known definition, in the operational approach, of the legality of including the organization/agency in the process (Fassin, 2009). Overall, if an organization/agency has all three attributes, it is considered as a definitive stakeholder, whose input is vital and is therefore more likely to be included in decision-making.

Understanding salient stakeholder identification processes and determining how to improve existing identification processes is useful for managers in preparing eco–tourism management plans through stakeholder participation. While improving the identification skills enables government agencies to apply the strategic approach successfully, Streib (1992) has identified several managerial functions, e.g. capable leadership within a strategic approach, supportive human resources, effective managerial skills in supporting strategic efforts with the availability of external support, and strategic efforts with minimum interference on internal processes. These managerial functions were later re–categorized into two major attributes in proving the decision-making process, personal development and change management (Marshak, 2005). More precisely, personal development involves strengthening the individual's capability in decision-making, while change management prepares a better decision making environment, which includes creating a better institutional framework and more effective procedures catering for the decision-making process.

4.3. Methodology

If the department wishes to shift to adopt a new approach to stakeholder identification, the existing approach must be fully understood, and adjustments made based upon these findings. Therefore, the objective of this study is to assess the usage of key constructs in identifying salient stakeholders and, later, to identify the causal factors that lead to this selection process. Improvement to the existing stakeholder identification approach is also examined. A mail questionnaire survey was conducted with the Forestry Departments, both at the Headquarters (Peninsular Malaysia) and at state forestry departments. Altogether, 129 questionnaires were collected. The respondents consisted mainly of managerial level staff, representing slightly more than half the number of potential respondents. In this questionnaire survey, respondents were required to answer the statements related to the sub-constructs of stakeholders' salient features, the influential factors on this selection process, and the preferred approach to improvement, based on a 5–point Likert scale.

For each key construct, multiple–item indicators were used to design the questionnaire, and each sub–construct or base consisted of four statements. In addition, there were 36 statements for the nine sub-constructs (or bases) that constitute salient features (Table 4.1). The key constructs and the numbers of sub-constructs used were legitimacy (12 items), power (16 items), and urgency (8 items). This framework followed the original idea of Mitchell *et al.* (1997), except for the sub-construct expert. The expert power was included as it was considered important in exercising administrative and managerial work requiring expert opinions. Furthermore, rich vocabulary and presentational technique would make a person more effective in negotiations with other stakeholders (Beritelli & Laesser, 2011; Driscoll & Crombie, 2001). Possessing higher level knowledge or expertise in fields related to the subject should be seen as an advantage. Managers with such an advantage would be able to manage natural resource–based tourism in areas requiring in–depth knowledge of natural sciences or the ability to deal with scientists (Lebel, Contreras, Pasong, & Garden, 2004). Thus, an expert sub–construct was added in this study.

Table 4.1 – Key issues used in designing hypothetical statements

No.	Key construct/Bases	Key issues highlighted
1	Legitimacy	
	Individual	Individual self-centred issues were given priority in management
	Organizational	Issues that are friendly to the organization were given priority in management
	Societal	Issues that met societal expectation were given priority in management
2	Power	
	Coercive	Able to make someone/something work by using a punitive approach
	Utilitarian	Able to make someone/something work by giving a reward
	Normative	Position that is socially acceptable, where such a position is able to influence someone/something to work accordingly
	Expert	Able to make someone/something work by applying their expert opinions to justify the reasons
3	Urgency	
	Time sensitivity	Issues that need to be handled within a short period of time were given priority
	Criticality	Issues that need to be handled as a priority because of their seriousness

The variables used in the model development needed to be statistically robust. A principal component analysis (PCA) was employed to determine the numbers of components within each key construct and the relevancy of these items within the three key constructs. In order to achieve this, the number of items for each key construct was reduced to an acceptable condition. Identifying these principal components helped to explain the correlations in each of the key constructs of stakeholders' salience. Any item whose inclusion in the construct was not statistically justified was dropped. The remaining items in each key construct were considered to be statistically consistent with that construct. Later, these statistically derived constructs were compared with the corresponding pre-determined constructs.

After determining the perception of forest managers on the three key constructs for stakeholder salience, the influential factors needed to be understood in order to improve the identification process. In the next analysis, a model linking salient features with influential factors and improvements was suggested. Attribution theory was applied to further understand the causal explanation for this identification process, and to determine whether internal (dispositional) or external (situational) factors had influenced managers' decisions. This basis was derived from research on Heider's theory related to determinants; internal (dispositional) versus external (situational) attributions that are possibly inferred as a person's attitude to a subject (Smith, 1994).

The distinctions between personal and situational causes were also highlighted in the attribution model. The circumstances enabled us to distinguish whether a person's choice was influenced by their personal preference or by the situation (organizational environment). This approach is usually applied to understanding social psychological phenomena in a working environment (Moore, 2000). For the purposes of this study, the internal attributes consisted of four items, and the external attributes of six items. The internal attributes included knowledge, working experience, and leadership style, while the external attributes included institutional procedures, focuses of organization, and the availability of required information. For the model on the causal selection of salient stakeholders' features, the structural equation modeling (SEM) was employed to perform the path analysis that examined the relationships between these variables.

A possible improvement was identified for the purpose of enhancing the stakeholder identification process in SEM. The preferred methods for improving the selection of salient stakeholders, according to the forest managers' perceptions, were identified. There were two ways of improving the process, either through human capital strengthening (2 items) or through changing the existing institutional system (5 items). In order for the forest managers and the administrators to manage efficiency and to become conscientious decision makers, they had to obtain broader views and interdisciplinary training (Henning, Abdullah, & Yip, 2007). The next generation of forest managers should possess not only technical skills but also be professionally competent in managing the forests and their stakeholders.

A number of factors are involved in setting up the platform for change in a public organization. These change management processes require a cooperative workforce team with an effective visionary leadership, which possesses an appropriate model of change, sufficient resources for negotiation and compromising, and well-planned and effective communication skills (Stewards & Kringas, 2003). Equally important, the high performance–based senior management that initially commits to the change should be retained (Boyne, James, John, & Petrovsky, 2011). In addition, some external political support should be in place for making such comprehensive changes to a public agency (Fernandez & Rainey, 2006). To sum up, this study proposed a model that included stakeholders' salience features, influential factors, and improvement approaches. The model was examined, and the relationship between its key variables was assessed.

Rules of thumb for verifying a SEM model (Schermelleh-Engel, Moosbrugger, & Müller, 2003) and cut-off criteria for selected fit indexes (Schreiber, Stage, King, Nora, & Barlow, 2006) were used to determine the acceptable range of the model. Besides these rules of thumb, a squared multiple correlation (R square) also gave some indication of the explanatory power of the data of this model. Similar to any multivariate model, a higher R square would indicate the greater explanatory power of the data set for that model. On top of using indexes and parameter estimations as verifiers of a model, researchers were cautioned by Schreiber *et al.* (2006) that end results must be theoretically sound rather than statistically modified. This is supported by Quintan and Maxwell (1999)'s argument that a statistical procedure is unable to detect specification errors. Statistically, a model might fit the sample data but give an incorrect representation of the population. Hence, researchers had to assess both technical issues concerning the study subject and the method that constructs this model to look for the possibility of a specification error, prior to carrying out the modeling analysis

4.4. Results

In the salient stakeholder identification process, emphasis was given to the stakeholder who has a legitimacy claim. In the pre-determined model, the sequent of selection is legitimacy (Mean, $M=3.86$), urgency ($M=3.83$) and power ($M=3.51$). This sequent did not alter even after obtaining the results from a statistically tested model; legitimacy ($M=3.76$) was still given greater priority as compared to power ($M=3.65$) and urgency ($M=3.71$). In normal circumstances, power was viewed as the most effective contributor to salience and as having more influence on the decision-making process, especially as regards stakeholders with social power who attempt to influence the decision-making process in public administration (Nicholson-Crotty & Nicholson-Crotty, 2004; Parent & Deephouse, 2007). However, the staff of Forestry Departments did not conform to this view. They insisted that legitimacy was the key factor in determining their stakeholders, as they perceived that the power of authority was still withheld by those stakeholders. The urgency sub–construct did not generate enough attention, even though it closely followed legitimacy. Generally speaking, people did not share views on urgency. Hence, a stakeholder was not treated as important if they only held an urgency claim (Neville, Bell, & Whitwell, 2011). If it was not their focal point (and they were therefore treated as stake–seekers), the managers might just ignore this issue.

In summary, the key construct of power was not chosen by the Forestry Department, even though it was considered more influential than the other two key constructs in identifying stakeholders. This suggests they might perceive themselves as having the power of authority in terms of eco–tourism development, whereas they are custodians of the forests and eco–tourism destinations. Ignorance of the fact that the state government was the higher authority to which they needed to refer regarding forest issues was prevalent. The Department needs to get approval and funding from the government for any forest development. As these three key constructs are equally important in salient stakeholder identification, the Department needs to review its stakeholder identification process if it wants to apply a strategic approach.

4.4.1. Influential factor and improvement

For the path analysis on the linkages between the salient features, influential factors and improvements, a statistically sound model ($R^2=0.37$) was presented (Figure 4.1). The model was able to capture certain aspects of the sample. Therefore, the model is presented, as it serves as a preliminary model of how causal factors and improvement are linked to salient stakeholders' features.

In this model, only the legitimacy (LEG) key construct was found to positively influence the selection of salient features (SAL). Key constructs power (POW) and urgency (URG) did not generate enough attention among the forest managers. They did not view these features as influential factors in their management practices. This is reflected in the earlier descriptive analysis, which investigated individual key constructs. The key construct legitimacy was more likely to be used to identify stakeholders. This indicates that the priority of this public agency is in its role as a law enforcer. However, this is also an obstacle to the application of a strategic approach. A paradigm shift among its managers is really needed from law enforcement to strategic planning.

In the same model, dispositional attributes (DIS; regression coefficient=0.42) were found to be better at influencing the selection of salient stakeholders than situational attributes (SIT; 0.16). In terms of dispositional factors, the lack of knowledge among forest managers in managing the relationships with other organizations was widely agreed to be one of the causes for failing to identify salient stakeholders. As for the improvement in stakeholder identification in terms of personal development, the dispositional approach (DISA; 0.39) had greater explanation power than the situational approach (SITA; 0.27). Personal development includes human capital strengthening to enable forest managers to be more competent in eco–tourism development planning. The forest managers, together with their support staff, must be highly competent in facing new challenges in a dynamic eco–tourism environment. Hence, they either need to upgrade the qualifications required to obtain administrative roles in the department for the purpose of managing stakeholders, or to provide in–service training to increase the capacity of existing human resources in executing this task.

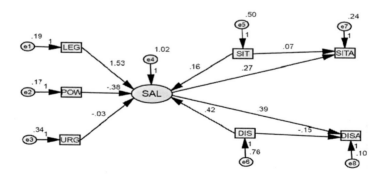

Figure 4.1 – Path analysis for suggested model

The managerial staff must develop the skills needed to handle other stakeholders; they no longer manage only the trees and the forests. They have to learn a creative way of facilitating the relationship between their departments and the stakeholders. This engagement process would be in line with the government policy of developing an effective delivery system that is more people–oriented. Engaging stakeholders and getting their feedback in order to improve the existing delivery system would enable image building for the government sector.

4.5. Conclusion

Public agencies such as the Forestry Department tend to identify stakeholders solely based upon legitimacy, and the sole use of this key construct derives from an operational approach. There is an indication that some managers do take urgency issues into consideration, but their preference remains for legitimacy when determining the salient features of stakeholders. If the Department wants to apply a strategic approach, they need to look again at the definition of legitimacy from a strategic management perspective, and also to include the other two key constructs (urgency and power) in the identification process. Due to the dynamism of the institutional environment, stakeholders may acquire other key constructs to strengthen their claims on stakes. Such possibilities as these should lead to urgent issues addressed by other stakeholders and also those who are only known to the manager as stake–seekers being reconsidered in the consultation process. Managers also need to be cautious with those who withhold power, as this could influence the decision-making process. Including all three key constructs could help to balance out the demands from various stakeholders to meet the criteria of sustainable eco–tourism destination, by considering more inputs prior to development.

This chapter has initiated a model that links salient stakeholder features with influential factors and potential improvement, using a quantitative approach. This result should suggest to the Department that human capital strengthening is needed to improve their staff's skills in identifying salient stakeholders. Since this model was only statistically sound, further studies are required to further investigate in greater detail the basis of each of the key constructs that together constitute the salient features of stakeholders. Additionally, diversifying the attributes used to determine the influential factors in the identification process and the improvement approach are suggested.

This chapter has also built a foundation for quantitative research into salient stakeholder identification. Future studies could examine those items used in constructing each key construct from various angles. This could be from the perspective of forest managers or other external organizations related to the field, e.g. environmental–based non-government organizations and tourism operators. Since this type of study concerns a dynamic environment, where relationships between stakeholders can change across time, researchers should have extensive knowledge of the study subject and related issues, and should follow recent trends and developments. Each case study has unique features, and such exclusivity must be addressed in the study. The decentralized management of forestry was duly recognized in this chapter. For other cases of eco–tourism development in such situations, evaluating the salient stakeholder identification process could be followed with minimal alterations to the contents of the research instrument.

References

Beritelli, P., & Laesser, C. (2011). Power dimensions and influence reputation in tourist destinations: empirical evidence from a network of actors and stakeholders. *Tourism Management*, 32, 1299-1309.

Boyne, G.A, James, O., John, P., & Petrovsky, N. (2011). Top management turnover and organizational performance: a test of a contingency model. *Public Administration Review*, 71(4), 572-581.

Colfer, C.J.P. (2005). *Who Counts Most in Sustainable Forest Management? CIFOR Working Paper No. 7.* Bogor, Indonesia: Center for International Forestry Research.

Currie, R.R., Seaton, S., & Wesley, F. (2009). Determining stakeholders for feasibility analysis. *Annals of Tourism Research*, 36(1), 41-63.

Driscoll, C., & Crombie, A. (2001). Stakeholder legitimacy management and the qualified good neighbour: the case of Nova Nada and JDI. *Business & Society*, 40(4), 442-471.

Fassin, Y. (2009). The stakeholder model refined. *Journal of Business Ethics*, 84, 113-135.

Fernandez, S., & Rainey, H.G. (2006). Managing successful organizational change in the public sector. *Public Administration Review*, 66(2), 168-176.

Freeman, R.E. (1984). *Strategic management: a stakeholder approach.* Boston: Pitman.

Henning, D.H., Abdullah, M., & Yip, H.W. (2007). Environmental administration for forester in-service training: raising consciousness and promoting good values. *The Malaysian Forester*, 70(1), 23-30.

Hurst, P. (1990). *Rainforest politics: ecological destruction in South-east Asia.* London: Zed.

King, B. (2008). A social movement perspective of stakeholder collective action and influence. *Business & Society*, 47(1), 21-49.

Krick, T., Forstater, M., Monaghan, P., & Sillanpää, M. (2005). *The stakeholder engagement manual (Volume 2): The practitioner's handbook on stakeholder engagement.* London: Accountability. Retrieved from http://www.accountability.org/about-us/publications/the-stakeholder.html

Lawrence, T.B., Wickins, D., & Philips, N. (1997). Managing legitimacy in ecotourism. *Tourism Management*, 18(5), 307-316.

Lebel, L., Contreras, A., Pasong, S., & Garden, P. (2004). Nobody know best: alternative perspectives on forest management and governance in Southeast Asia. *International Environmental Agreements: Politics, Law and Economics*, 4, 111-127.

Lindberg, K., Furze, B., Staff, M., & Black, R. (1997). *Ecotourism and other services derived from forests in the Asia-Pacific region: outlook to 2010. Asia-Pacific Forestry Sector Outlook Study Working Paper Series No: 24.* Bangkok: FAO.

Marshak, R.J. (2005). Contemporary challenges to the philosophy and practice of organization development. In D.L. Bradford & W.W. Burke (eds.). *Reinventing organization development: The change agent series for groups and organizations* (pp.19-42). San Francisco: Pfeiffer.

Mitchell, R.K., Agle, B.R., Chrisman, J.J., & Spence, L.J. (2011). Toward a theory of stakeholder salience in family firms. *Business Ethics Quarterly*, 21(2), 235-255.

Mohd, R., & Yaman, A.R. (2001). *Overview of forest law enforcement in Peninsular Malaysia.* Petaling Jaya, Malaysia: WWF Malaysia.

Moore, J.E. (2000). Why is this happening? A causal attribution approach to work exhaustion consequences. *Academy of Management Review*, 25(2), 335-349.

Neville, B.A., Bell, S.J., & Whitwell, G.J. (2011). Stakeholder salience revisited: Refining, redefining, and refueling an underdeveloped conceptual tool. *Journal of Business Ethics*, 102, 357-378.

Nicholson-Crotty, S., & Nicholson-Crotty, J. (2004). Interest group influence on managerial priorities in public organizations. *Journal of Public Administration Research and Theory*, 14(4), 571-583.

Parent, M.M., & Deephouse, D.L. (2007). A case study of stakeholder identification and prioritization by managers. *Journal of Business Ethnics*, 75, 1-23.

PEMANDU (2010). *Economic transformation programme: the roadmap.* Putrajaya, Malaysia: PEMANDU.

Quintana, S.M., & Maxwell, S.E. (1999). Implications of recent developments in structural equation modeling for counseling psychology. *The Counseling Psychologist*, 27(4), 485-527.

Primmer, E., & Kyllönen, S. (2006). Goals for public participation implied by sustainable development, and the preparatory process of the Finnish National Forest Programme. *Forest Policy and Economics*, 8, 838-853.

Schermelleh-Engel, K., Moosbrugger, H., & Müller, H. (2003). Evaluating the fit of structural equation models: tests of significance and descriptive goodness-of-fit measures. *Methods of Psychological Research Online*, 8(2), 23-74.

Schreiber, J.B., Stage, F.K., King, J., Nora, A., & Barlow, E.A. (2006). Reporting structural equation modelling and confirmatory factor analysis results: a review. *The Journal of Educational Research*, 99(6), 323-337.

Simpson, K. (2001). Strategic planning and community involvement as contributors to sustainable tourism development. *Current Issues in Tourism*, 4(1), 3-41.

Sinha, P.C. (2006). *Global tourism, sustainable tourism & eco-tourism: code of ethics, charter, guidelines, resolutions.* New Delhi: SBS Publishers & Distributors.

Smith, E.R. (1994). Social cognition contributions to attribution theory and research. In P.G. Devine, D.L. Hamilton, & T.M. Ostrom (eds.). *Social cognition: impact on social psychology* (pp.77-108). San Diego: Academic Press.

Streib, G. (1992). Applying strategic decision making in local government. *Public Productivity & Management Review*, 15(3), 341-354.

Stewards, J., & Kringas, P. (2003). Change management – strategy and values in six agencies from the Australian public services. *Public Administration Review*, 63(6), 675-688.

Winn, M.I. (2001). Building stakeholder theory with a decision modeling methodology. *Business & Society*, 40(2), 133-166.

Yasmi, Y., Broadhead, J., Enters, T., & Genge, C. (2010). *Forestry policies, legislation and institutions in Asia and the Pacific: trends and emerging needs for 2020.* RAP Publication 2010/10. Bangkok: FAO.

Yip, H.W., Abdullah M., Wan Razali, W.M., Manohar M., & Awang Noor A.G. (2012). Strategic approach in stakeholder identification for sustainable ecotourism development. *The Malaysian Foresters*, 75(2), 147-158.

Zietsma, C., & Winn, M.I. (2008). Building chains and directing flows: strategies and tactics of mutual influence in stakeholder conflicts. *Business & Society*, 47(1), 68-101.

CHAPTER FIVE

STAKEHOLDER MAPPING AS A TOOL FOR TOURISM POLICY IMPLEMENTATION IN MEXICO

ISMAEL M. RODRÍGUEZ–HERRERA AND JUAN IGNACIO PULIDO–FERNÁNDEZ

Abstract

This chapter develops an approach to tourism policy implementation based on stakeholder mapping which contributes to the improvement of destination management. This proposal helps to identify the main actors involved in the tourism development of any destination and the role played by each of them in this process, as well as the relations existing among them. The proposed methodology has been applied in the town of Comala (México), which is a tourism destination included in the programme *Pueblos Mágicos de México* (Magical Towns of Mexico). Through this programme, the Mexican government is trying to increase the value of tourism resources and strengthen the social capital of some municipalities.
Keywords: tourism policy, stakeholder mapping, destination management, stakeholder theory, Mexico.

5.1 Introduction

Relevant topics such as collaboration, cooperation and association in the context of tourism development and management have been widely discussed in the scientific literature during the last two decades. As stated by Bramwell and Lane (1999, p.179), this reflects a trend that was first observed in a wider political context in which many governments, mainly of developed countries, became aware of the problems arising from the lack of connection and understanding not only within tourism but also between the public and private sectors.

Since the mid–1990s, some researchers began to relate the then recent Stakeholder Theory to the tourism phenomenon. As a result, the first research works linking these two aspects appeared (Jamal & Getz, 1995; Palmer & Bejou, 1995; Robson & Robson, 1996). Since then, numerous works have been published in which Stakeholder Theory has been applied to the analysis of very diverse issues, ranging from collaborative planning and conflict management to governance and sustainable management of resources, and even tourism management of cultural heritage or protected areas.

The participation of all stakeholders in the process of planning and management of any tourism destination requires, as a first step, their identification and, specially, the delimitation of the relationship between them. Therefore, a change, no matter how slight, in the conditions under which this relationship is developed will, to a greater or lesser extent, determine the structure of the model, which will have to adapt quickly to the new circumstances in order to maintain the possibility of achieving the proposed objectives. This constant adaptation requires, thus, timely and accurate information on stakeholders and their interrelationship.

Consequently, the objective of this chapter is to demonstrate that it is possible to identify the main actors involved in the tourism development of any destination, as well as to define the role played by each actor in this process and the relationship between them. This will contribute to the subsequent development of a tourism policy that will generate the proper environment and necessary incentives to improve the relationship between the actors involved, which will also improve destination management.

The first part of this work is devoted to an overview of the main contributions on Stakeholder Analysis, which are interesting due to their possible application within the framework of tourism destination planning and management. Then, an application of this analysis is provided by means of a case study (the town of Comala, Mexico), which examines stakeholders' relation to the tourism development of this Mexican tourism destination that is included in the *Pueblos Mágicos* Programme. Finally, the conclusions drawn are discussed.

5.2 Literature Review

The term "stakeholder" has its origins in the work of Freeman (1984; 1994) on strategic management of business organisations. According to this author, stakeholders are defined as "any group or individual who can affect or is affected by the achievement of the organisation's objectives" (Freeman, 1984, p.46). Since then, various authors (such as Atkinson *et al.*, 1997; Clarkson, 1995; Donaldson & Preston, 1995; Freeman *et al.*, 2004; Friedman & Miles, 2002; Frooman, 1999; Harrison & Freeman, 1999; Jones, 1995; Mitchell & Cohen, 2006; Mitchell *et al.*, 1997; Scott & Lane, 2000; Wood & Jones, 1995) made contributions that added to the body of scientific literature known today as Stakeholder Theory. This theory emphasises the importance of considering the diverse actors involved in order to be able to achieve the set objectives.

Grimble *et al.* (1995, p.3-4) define the concept of "stakeholder analysis" (hereafter referred to as SA), as "a method to understand a system by identifying its key actors or stakeholders and assessing their respective interest in the system in question".

Recent tourism literature reflects a growing interest in SA. From the perspective of Stakeholder Theory, tourism destinations can be considered as open systems involving numerous (private and public) and interdependent (any action in one part affects all other parts) actors. There are many different agents involved and affected by the development of any destination (Medeiros de Araujo & Bramwell, 1999; Sheehan & Ritchie, 2005), so it is necessary to guarantee that all of them are involved in its planning, management and commercialisation (Bramwell & Lane, 1999; Jamal & Getz, 1995; Keogh, 1990; Timothy, 1998). In this context, a good part of scientific contributions consider cooperation and collaboration as key elements for the planning of tourism destinations (Aas *et al.*, 2005; Bramwell & Sharman, 1999; Hall, 1999; Ladkin & Bertramini, 2001). Nowadays, the relevance of collaboration in planning has become undeniable. There is, thus, an increasing need for tourism planning and management processes to facilitate the informed and active participation of all persons, institutions and organisations which, in one way or another, affect or are affected by the tourism development of any destination.

In the area of tourism, Jamal and Getz (1995, p.188) describe "stakeholder collaboration" as "a process of joint decision-making among key stakeholders of an inter–organisational community tourism domain to resolve planning problems of the domain and/or manage issues related to the planning and development of the domain". Based on this concept, different researchers (Aas *et al.*, 2005; Bornhorst el at. 2010; Dredge, 2006; Jamal & Getz, 1995; Sautter & Leisen, 1999; Selin & Beason, 1991; Timothy, 1998; Yüksel *et al.*, 2005) have been developing a set of approaches to cooperation mechanisms that facilitate a collaborative approach between stakeholders in the processes of decision-making in tourism destinations. In this way, destination planning and management actions would make it possible to accommodate diverse and even conflicting interests.

Likewise, progress has been made in the analysis of the advantages and disadvantages of collaboration among stakeholders (Aas *et al.*, 2005; Bramwell & Sharman, 1999; Medeiros de Araujo & Bramwell, 1999). But, most of the progress made in the recent years, especially, has concerned the possibilities that this type of analysis offers for destination network management. In fact, Meriläinen and Lemmetyinen (2011, p.28) point out that "the coordination of cooperation seems to focus on the actor whereas strategic management approaches the action from the perspective of the whole network". Therefore, it is possible to improve the management of tourism destinations by strengthening the relational dynamics of stakeholders, which requires a suitable tourism policy that contributes to generate the proper environment and necessary incentives for all stakeholders to negotiate, discuss and, finally, cooperate to achieve the set objectives.

Dredge (2006) affirms that there are different levels of political support for the different tourism issues and recognises that the role, power, interactions and functions of the network's members can vary. Therefore, SA can be used to understand the "chaos" or the complexity of the network of actors that make up a destination. This highlights the importance of examining not only the structural aspects, but also those social or cultural aspects that are less tangible, adopting a qualitative approach.

5.3 Case study

Despite recent trends in the tourism flows, Mexico City is still one of the top tourism destinations worldwide, and this activity constitutes the fundamental driving force of its economy. Nevertheless, its dependence on the sun and sand tourism segment has led the government to look for greater offer diversification in order to become more competitive.

In this regard, one of the federal programmes aimed at boosting tourism in new destinations has been the so-called *Pueblos Mágicos* Programme. According to the information obtained from the Mexican Ministry of Tourism (SECTUR) official webpage, this programme is developed by this Ministry in collaboration with other governmental authorities at national and municipal level and "contributes to enhance the value of a group of towns of this country that have always been prominent in the Mexican imaginary. They offer fresh and different alternatives to national and foreign visitors. It is more than a rescue; it is an acknowledgment to those who inhabit those beautiful places all over

Mexico and have managed to keep their cultural and historical wealth" (SECTUR, 2009, p.1).

Comala, located in the state of Colima and included in the previously mentioned programme, is the particular tourism destination that will be analysed in this paper. Comala is only 6 km away from the capital city and it has an area of 254 km^2; it is located 600 meters above sea level. The predominant climate is sub-humid and warm, with a rainy summer and an annual average temperatures ranging from 23 °C to 27 °C.

According to the 2010 Population and Housing Census published by INEGI[1], this municipality has 20,888 inhabitants, with almost the same number of men and women. The population pyramid shows that most of the population are between 25 and 59 years old, so the predominant age group is adults. In 2010, the number of people economically active was 9,012, 33.3% of them were employed in the primary sector, 24.2% in the secondary sector and 41.2% in the tertiary sector.

The offer of accommodation services in the town of Comala is limited, but singular. It has one five-star hotel, with 25 rooms, and 17 other tourism establishments that are not classified into any accommodation category, which offer 84 rooms in large old houses. In contrast, the restaurant services are sufficient and attractive, with 31 establishments that offer typical local cuisine.

Tourism arrivals in the town of Comala are largely explained by its proximity to the capital city, which makes it an ideal weekend destination. Yet, it shows a significant increase in tourism demand during Easter, summer and December holidays. In this region, the average length of stay is 2 days and the average daily expenditure per tourist is 575 MXN (pesos). In 2007, the average hotel occupancy rate was 49%.

A *Pueblo Mágico* (Magical Town) is "a town with symbolic attributes, legends, history, significant events, daily life, in short, *magic* that emanates from each one of its social and cultural manifestations, and which nowadays means a great opportunity for tourism development" (SECTUR, 2009, p.1).

In June of 2014, this programme comprised 83 towns distributed across the country. Over the more than ten years of this programme, the results obtained have been analysed and adjustments have been made. In 2009, the rules for the operation of the programme were presented, which highlighted the need to create the so-called *Pueblo Mágico* Committees[2] (hereafter referred to as PMC), in which local communities should play a leading role.

The impact of this programme has varied from one destination to another. Therefore, this paper aims to analyse the extent to which tourism development affects, or is affected, by the relationships between stakeholders in a tourism destination.

5.4. Methodology

In order to achieve the set objective, a methodology has been elaborated that enables Stakeholder Mapping (hereafter referred to as SM), which has the objective of identifying and characterising stakeholders in the selected tourism destinations. In turn, this will help to address those aspects which, by means of tourism policies, must be reinforced to guarantee stakeholders' participation in destination management, as well as to generate greater relational dynamics, where necessary. SM can be defined as "a type of stakeholder analysis that focuses on the assessment of a large number of actors linked together by various forms of relationships" (Mehrizi *et al.*, 2009, p.429). In short, as these authors claim, SM tries to determine the links between the different actors, their objectives, actions or responsibilities, and the institutions that regulate the interactions among them. This study proposes an analysis framework consisting of four steps, described as follows:

Step 1 Analysis of the social, demographic and tourism aspects of each destination: The first step in examining these destinations involved a thorough analysis of the general characteristics on the town. Using complementary information, this analysis focused on socioeconomic aspects, while also taking into account other elements such as location, accessibility, tourism supply and demand, among others[3].

Step 2 Survey of key actors: Having established the context, it was easier to make a preliminary identification of local tourism-related actors. The identification of the key actors in all cases was based on non-probability chain sampling or network (snowball) sampling. Eventually, fieldwork began with semi-structured interviews with the *Pueblos Mágicos de México* programme managers conducted at national tourism institutions' headquarters. Thus, a first approach to the tourism development of the town studied was obtained, along with a preliminary list of actors within that destination. Afterwards, the information obtained was verified and further supplemented by data collected from a key informant at the study site. Considering the above, the universe of tourism actors related to the destination was determined. On this basis, those actors to whom the survey instrument designed would be applied were chosen, taking into account that in this type of study (qualitative), sample size is not important from a probabilistic point of view. This is due to the fact that the most important factor in this kind of research is the depth of data collected. Therefore, the emphasis is on the quality of the sample rather than the quantity of respondents. In this sense, this research required actors that could be helpful in order to understand the studied phenomenon (Hernandez *et al.*, 2008). The criteria for the application of the survey instruments developed include being a member of the *Pueblos Mágicos* Committee and/or being a key actor in the tourism development of the destination. For a more complete analysis, in addition to the interviews, it was decided to use another instrument, based on the analysis of other previously developed instruments (Arriagada *et al.*, 2004). Besides, in order to complete the analysis, that instrument was enhanced by adding elements from Stakeholder Theory, which allowed a deeper insight into the relationships among actors and their interactions. The information obtained made it possible to elaborate a map of tourism actors.

Step 3 Application of the model: For the purposes of this research, the analysis and methodology suggested by Mitchell *et al.* (1997) is particularly interesting. These authors make a proposal for the identification and characterisation of stakeholders based on the analysis of twenty-seven definitions of the term stakeholder. They are classified according to three specific attributes: power, legitimacy and urgency. Then, these attributes are combined and eight different groups of stakeholders are defined. The cornerstones of Stakeholder Theory on which the development of this model is based were perfectly systematised by these authors, so readers interested in further details on this topic are referred to their paper (Mitchell *et al.*, 1997, p. 869). In relation to the attributes proposed for stakeholders, the authors highlight the following considerations: 1) they may vary, which implies that they are subject to change at any time; 2) they are socially constructed, so the degree or existence of each attribute can be subjective, as they depend on multiple perceptions; and 3) consciousness and choice may or may not occur, in other words, an actor may or may not be conscious of possessing an attribute (Mitchell *et al.*, 1997, p.868). The combination of the three attributes (Mitchell *et al.*, 1997, p.872) allows the identification of different stakeholder groups: those with only one attribute (called *latent* stakeholders), those exhibiting two attributes (called *expectant* stakeholders) and those possessing three attributes (called *definitive* stakeholders). Each typology proposed shows different characteristics, which have different effects on the management, in this case, of a tourism destination. There is also another group which, with no attributes, are not considered as stakeholders. Although the theoretical proposal developed by Mitchell *et al.* (1997) is focused on the business area, its application to tourism management provides a qualitative view of great importance to understand the social dynamics in a certain destination, which facilitates the identification and analysis of social capital in that site. This methodology has already been successfully applied to the classification and study of stakeholders in tourism destinations (Currie *et al.*, 2009; Montanari & Staniscia, 2010; Pulido-Fernandez, 2010). For our study, a variant of the analysis of stakeholder attributes proposed by Mitchell et al. (1997) was incorporated. The analysis has been addressed from two perspectives: first, all members of the PMC were asked about their perceptions of themselves in relation to each of the three attributes proposed by the above theory (power, legitimacy and urgency); second, all respondents (not only the PMC members) were asked to assess these same attributes in relation to those actors involved in the management of the tourism destination under study with whom they are in contact.

Step 4 Identification of the tourism policy issues to be addressed: The application of this analysis has provided a clear overview of the impacts, from a relational point of view, resulting from the implementation of the programme in this destination and of the role that each stakeholder, and particularly each member of the PMC, plays in its tourism management. This has allowed us to make very specific recommendations for actions that should be taken to improve relational dynamics in this destination.

5.5. Results

The results obtained from the study are now presented. In order to do this, a distinction will be made between the two previously mentioned perspectives: actors' perceptions of themselves and actors' perceptions of other actors. The results concerning the self-perception of the stakeholders that are members of the PMC in the town of Comala regarding power, legitimacy and urgency attributes are graphically represented in Figure 5.1. As can be observed, there are two actors who consider that they possess the three attributes: the president of the PMC and the representative of the travel agency sector. Therefore, they define themselves as definitive stakeholders, while the representative of the accommodation sector does not claim to possess any of the three attributes mentioned, so she does not consider herself as a stakeholder. Apart from these, there are two latent actors who affirmed to possess only one attribute: actor 9, who represents the crafts sector and regard him/herself as possessing the attribute of power, classified as an inactive stakeholder. Next, representing the town council, actor 2, who attributed himself only the attribute of legitimacy, is classified as a discretionary stakeholder.

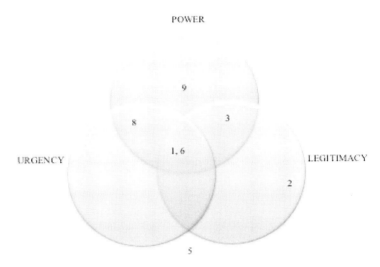

Figure 5.1 – Typology of stakeholders, members of PMC

Moreover, two stakeholders are identified and defined as expectant due to the fact that they possess two attributes: actor 8, who represents the sector of construction professionals and claims to have the attributes of urgency and power, which theory defines as dangerous, as these attributes could be used to support their own demands; and actor 3, the representative of the national tourism office, who is defined as a dominant stakeholder because of possessing the attributes of power and legitimacy.

However, the most interesting data were obtained from the interviews carried out with the actors. They were asked to assess the attributes of other actors with whom they are in contact regarding Comala's tourism management (Figure 5.2). Other actors' assessment of the attributes that the members of the PMC possess showed mixed results. Thus, the PMC includes definitive (4), discretionary (4) and independent (2) stakeholders.

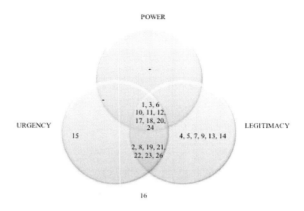

Figure 5.2 – Typology of stakeholders in Comala

As the results show, there is an important group that includes ten actors showing the three attributes. Therefore, they are considered as definitive stakeholders. This group includes those actors who considered themselves to have the three attributes, the representative of the national tourism office, a local opinion leader, the director of the University Museum, the owner of an accommodation establishment, the adviser to PMC, the municipal director of public works, a university professor and the Federal tourism officer. Thus, all of them are key actors in the tourism management of the destination, although it is significant that they are not always considered to be part of the formal structure that supports this programme.

There is another important group of actors, identified in Figure 5.2 as dependent, which include seven stakeholders that are considered to possess the attributes of urgency and legitimacy. The actors identified within this group are the following: the representative of the town council, the representative of local architects, of the union of poncheros[4], of bakers; scholars in general, as well as the representative of CDI[5]. Furthermore, within the group of discretionary stakeholders, we identified four PMC members, the president of the civil association "Grupo Comala" and an hotelier.

FONATUR is also identified as a dominant actor, as it possesses both power and legitimacy, while a cultural promoter was identified as a demanding actor, as it was only associated with the attribute of urgency. Finally, there was only one actor to whom no attributes were ascribed, who, therefore, is not considered as a stakeholder.

This detailed overview of relational dynamics in this destination shows the need to encourage the participation of all tourism-related actors, belonging or not belonging to the PMC, as well as the need to reinforce the communication channels between the different actors.

These results must be considered in the design and implementation of the tourism policy instruments. On the one hand, there are stakeholders to whom other actors ascribe the three attributes and, therefore, they are essential for the management of the destination. However, they are not part of the organisation in which projects are discussed and they are not able to propose new actions. Consequently, it is urgent to change the membership of the PMC so that they can be given the opportunity to become part of this group.

On the other hand, it is confirmed that some stakeholders have not assumed the role that others assign to them and, as a consequence, their expertise and skills are being underutilised. Therefore, it would be convenient to develop actions aimed at making people aware of the importance of involving these actors to a greater extent in destination development and management processes.

Finally, there are stakeholders who show self-ascribed attributes that others do not ascribe to them. Yet, they have been ascribed certain attributes that they have not been able to identify for themselves. Consequently, it may be concluded that relational dynamics are still unstable in this destination, which is clearly affecting its tourism development process. Therefore, it is necessary to reinforce these relational dynamics, which would eventually promote good governance.

5.6. Conclusion

This chapter proposes a new instrument to analyse stakeholders. So far, SA has been mainly used in the formulation of policies. Here, we have made an effort to demonstrate its potential as a tool for evaluating public policies in order to promote tourism development. SA has been developed based on structural view of policy analysis. However, when trying to link actors to policies and objectives through action plans, it has been demonstrated that it is possible to combine a behavioural and structural approach in a coherent way, through stakeholder mapping.

The methodology proposed allows researchers to easily identify stakeholders within an analysed destination and assess the role they play in the tourism management of their town. In addition, the use of this type of analysis helps to find cases in which it is necessary to adjust tourism policies to the actual reality of the destination. Therefore, an approach to

SA similar to the one developed in this study could be used for different analytical and practical purposes.

To conclude, there are many similarities between these results and those found in the literature on this topic, mainly regarding the need to consider new debates on quality of participation and links among actors as tourism development consolidates. Thus, as stated by Pulido-Fernández (2010), the participation of stakeholders is a determining factor that guarantees the effectiveness of tourism destination planning and management. This research also shows that, through the use of tools such as Stakeholder Theory, it is possible to identify the different actors engaged in this process and define their interests and interrelations.

As can be observed, SA is an effective tool to identify the actors in a tourism destination, as well as to determine the role they play in management and eventually assess current relations among them. All this is essential for an adequate promotion of good tourism governance policies aimed at destination management improvement.

References

Aas, C., Ladkin, A., & Fletcher, J. (2005). Stakeholder collaboration and heritage management. *Annals of Tourism Research,* 32(1), 28-48.

Arriagada, I., Miranda, F., & Pávez, T. (2004). *Lineamientos de acción para el diseño de programas de superación de la pobreza desde el enfoque del capital social. Guía conceptual y metodológica.* Santiago de Chile: CEPAL.

Atkinson, A., Waterhouse, J., & Wells, R. (1997). A stakeholder approach to strategic performance measurement. *Sloan Management Review,* 38(3), 25-37.

Bornhorst, T., Ritchie, J., & Sheehan, L. (2010). Determinants of tourism success for DMOs & destinations: An empirical examination of stakeholders perspectives. *Tourism Management,* 31, 572-589.

Bramwell, B., & Lane, B. (1999). Collaboration and partnerships for sustainable tourism. *Journal of Sustainable Tourism,* 7(3&4), 179-181.

Bramwell, B., & Sharman, A. (1999). Collaboration in local tourism policymaking. *Annals of Tourism Research,* 26(2), 392-415.

Clarkson, M. (1995). A stakeholders framework for analyzong and evaluating corporate social performance. *Academy of Management Review,* 20(1), 92-117.

Currie, R., Seaton, S., & Wesley, F. (2009). Determining stakeholders for feasibility analisis. *Annals of Tourism Research,* 36(1), 41-63.

Donaldson, T., & Preston, L. (1995). The stakeholder theory of the corporation: Concepts, evidence, and implications. *Academy of Management Review*, 20(1), 65-91.

Dredge, D. (2006). Policy networks and the local organization of tourism. *Tourism Management*, 27(2), 269-280.

Freeman, R. (1984). *Strategic management: A stakeholder approach.* Boston: Pitman.

—. (1994). The politics of stakeholder theory: Some future directions. *Business Ethics Quartely*, 4(4).

Freeman, R., Wicks, A., & Parmar, B. (2004). Stakeholder theory and "The Corporate Objetive Revisited". *Organization Science*, 15(3), 364-369.

Friedman, A., & Miles, S. (2002). Developing stakeholder theory. *Journal of Management Studies*, 39(1), 1-21.

Frooman, J. (1999). Stakeholder influence strategies. *Academy of Management Review*, 24(2), 191-205.

Grimble, R., Chan, M., Aglionby, J., & Quan, J. (1995). *Trees and trade-offs: A stakeholders approach to natural resource management.* Gatekeeper Series, vol. 52. London: IIED.

Hall, M. (1999). Rethinking collaboration and partnership: A public policy perspective. *Journal of Sustainable Tourism*, 7(3&4), 274-289.

Harrison, J., & Freeman, R. (1999). Stakeholder, social responsability, and performance: Empirical evidence and theoretical perspectives. *Academy of Management Review*, 42(5), 479-485.

Hernández, R., Fernández, C., & Baptista, P. (2008). *Metodología de la investigación* (Cuarta ed.). México: McGraw-Hill Interamericana Editores.

Jamal, T., & Getz, D. (1995). Collaboration theory and community tourism planning. *Annals of Tourism Research*, 22(1), 186-204.

Jones, T. (1995). Instrumental Stakeholders theory: A sinthesis of ethics and economis. *Academy of Management Review*, 20, 404-437.

Keogh, B. (1990). Public participation in community tourism planning. *Annals of Tourism Research*, 17, 449-465.

Ladkin, A., & Bertramini, A. (2001). Collaborative tourism planning: A case study of Cusco, Peru. *Current Issues in Tourism*, 5(2), 71-93.

Medeiros de Araujo, L., & Bramwell, B. (1999). Stakeholder assessment and collaborative tourism planning: The case of Brazil´s Costa Dourada Project. *Journal of Sustainable Tourism*, 7(3&4), 356-378.

Mehrizi, M., Ghasemzadeh, F., & Molas-Gallart, J. (2009). Stakeholder mapping as an assessment framework for policy implementation. *Evaluation*, 15(4), 427-444.

Meriläinen, K., & Lemmetyinen, A. (2011). Destination network management: A conceptual analysis. *Tourism Review*, 66(3), 25-31.

Mitchell, R., & Cohen, B. (2006). Stakeholder theory and the entrepreneurial firm. *Journal of Small Business Strategy*, 17(1), 1-15.

Mitchell, R., Agle, B., & Wood, D. (1997). Toward a theory of a stakeholders identification and salience: defining the principle of who and what really counts. *Academy of Management Review*, 22(4), 853-886.

Montanari, A., & Staniscia, B. (2010). Rome: A difficult path between tourist pressure and sustainable development. *Rivista di Scienze del Turismo*, 2, 301-316.

Palmer, A., & Bejou, D. (1995). Tourism destination marketing alliances. *Annals of Tourism Research*, 22(3), 616-629.

Pulido-Fernández, J.I. (2010). Las partes interesadas en la gestión turística de los parques naturals andaluces. Identificación de interrelaciones e intereses. *Revista de Estudios Regionales*, 88, 147-175.

Pulido-Fernández, J.I., & Rodríguez-Herrera, I.M. (2011). El programa Pueblos Mágicos de México como promotor del desarrollo local. Una revisión de la política pública al desarrollo turístico. In J. Juárez, & B. Ramírez, (Coords.) *Turismo rural en México. Complemento o exclusión en el desarrollo territorial rural* (pp.52-86). Puebla: Colegio de Posgraduados.

Robson, J., & Robson, I. (1996). From shareholders to stakeholders: Critical issues for tourism marketers. *Tourism Management*, 17(7), 533-540.

Sautter, E., & Leisen, B. (1999). Managing stakeholders. A tourism planning model. *Annals of Tourism Research*, 26(2), 312-328.

Scott, S., & Lane, V. (2000). A stakeholder approach to organizational identity. *Academy of Management Review*, 25(1), 43-52.

SECTUR. 2009. *Pueblos Mágicos. Reglas de operación*. Disponible en linea en: http://www.sectur.gob.mx/work/sites/sectur/resources/LocalContent/15142/20/Reglas_de_operacion.pdf

Selin, S., & Beason, K. (1991). Interorganizational relations in tourism. *Annals of Tourism Research*, 18, 639-652.

Sheehan, L., & Ritchie, B. (2005). Destination stakeholders: Exploring identity and salience. *Annlas of Tourism Research*, 32(3), 711-734.

Timothy, D. (1998). Cooperative tourism planning in a developing destination. *Journal of Sustainable Tourism*, 6(1), 52-68.

Wood, D., & Jones, R. (1995). Stakeholder mismatching: A theoretical problem in empirical research on corporate social performance. *Journal of Organizational Analysis,* 3(3), 229-267.

Yüksel, F., Bramwell, B., & Yüksel, A. (2005). Centralized and decentralized tourism governance in Turkey. *Annals of Tourism Research,* 32(4), 859-886.

Notes

[1] Mexico's National Institute for Statistics and Geography. Available in http://www.inegi.org.mx

[2] These committees have the function of being the representatives between government levels and the local population. They are also agencies for the consultation and analysis for tourism projects that will be submitted to the Secretariat of Federal Tourism (SECTUR, 2009, p.16).

[3] For a detailed overview of the type of analysis performed in each one of the destinations included in this programme, see Pulido-Fernandez and Rodriguez-Herrera (2011).

[4] In this town, name given to the people who work in the production and sale of "ponche", which is a typical local beverage.

[5] National Commission for the Development of the Indigenous Peoples (Public Organisation).

Chapter Six

Developing Strategies and Overcoming Barriers for the 'Dubai Tourism Vision 2020'

Esmat Zaidan

Abstract

Massive investments in newly built high–quality tourism attractions have made Dubai one of the world's leading international tourist destinations and the fastest growing in the world. This chapter examines the strategies that should be developed by Dubai tourism planners to achieve the 'Dubai Tourism Vision 2020' of attracting 20 million visitors annually. It also identifies the main strengths, opportunities, and barriers that the city has to overcome. Primary data was collected by conducting interviews with tourism planners in Dubai. SWOT analysis has been conducted. The principal strengths, weaknesses, threats, and opportunities of the tourism planning initiative to achieve the 'Dubai Tourism Vision 2020' have been identified. Barriers must be overcome before opportunities can be fully exploited. **Keywords**: tourism vision, sustainable tourism, tourism planning, SWOT analysis, cultural tourism, United Arab Emirates.

6.1. Introduction

As a major city-emirate in the United Arab Emirates (UAE), Dubai is widely recognised as one of the top tourism destinations not only in the Middle East but the world. Apart from its oil, the UAE has generated huge revenues from its tourism industry in Dubai. Rapid modernisation and Westernisation as a main approach for tourism development have positioned Dubai at the top of the global tourism destination map. With ambitions to become the most visited tourist destination worldwide, Dubai, a state with small territories and limited natural and cultural tourism resources (Stephenson, 20143) but relatively wealthy, has been spending billions of dollars to build an outstanding modern city almost from scratch in less than 20 years (Bageen, 2007).

Forty years ago, the UAE was one of the least developed regions in the world (Sharpley, 2008). Traditional societal structures in the UAE consisted of familial leadership, limited collaboration with Western society or even most Middle Eastern societies, and a nomadic subsistence economy and culture (Heard-Bey, 2005). Modernity, including decisions to move toward a tourism-focused economy, has altered these realities. Since the mid–1980s, the tourism sector in Dubai has experienced the most rapid growth of any economic sector in Dubai; correspondingly, Dubai has become one of the fastest growing tourist destinations in the world (Henderson, 2006).

With the UAE taking significant steps in diversifying its economy to increase the non-oil sector's contribution to Gross Domestic Product (GDP) by the year 2030, Dubai has effectively employed its strategic plan to diversify and reinforce its oil-dependent economy, with the tourism industry evolving as an extraordinarily successful core sector (Sharpley, 2008). Dubai has already developed to the point where oil accounts for only 7% of the emirate's GDP. Today, tourism comprisesnearly 25% of the emirate's annual GDP (Henderson, 2008). In 2012, for example, Dubai gained US$10.4bn as revenue from its tourism sector (Khaleej Times, 2013). The most obvious and publicised outcome of tourism development in Dubai has been the intense and ongoing increase in the supply of high-quality tourism infrastructure, such as accommodation facilities, attractive tourist attractions and other development projects (Sharpley, 2008). The most ambitious projects include a US$3 billion construction scheme to overcome the lack of natural beaches in Dubai by building man-made islands: the Palm Jumeirah has the form of a palm tree with a trunk and 17 fronds; another is an archipelago that forms a kind of map of the world. These islands have added more than 60 km of coastline to the emirate (Economic Intelligence Unit, 2003). The islands are linked to the mainland by beautiful causeways which serve thousands of luxury villas, a range of hotels, such as Atlantis, and other attractive tourism facilities. Such significant development projects are controlled principally by state-owned development companies and Emaar (30% owned by the Dubai government) and they are working towards achieving Sheikh Mohammed's vision of Dubai as the ultimate innovative tourism destination in the world (Sharpley, 2008).

Accordingly, Dubai has transformed its urban landscape and image into a mixed-use urban development containing luxury residences, extensive shopping complexes, tall skyscrapers, luxury hotels (such as the iconic Burj Al Arab hotel), immense malls, inventive theme parks, international events, and a variety of entertainment complexes (Smith, 2010).Another unique high-profile scheme for the small desert emirate includes 'Ski Dubai', an indoor ski slope located inside the Dubai Mall, which itself is the largest shopping mall in the world; 'Snow World' is an indoor ski resort with an artificial mountain, a four-star ski lodge and, cable cars. According to Economic Intelligence Unit (2003), this ski resort uses snow cannons to cover a 3,500 ft. ski slope. The increasing number of tourist arrivals is also due to Dubai tourism events such as the Dubai Shopping Festival that made the city a global brand, and the Dubai Summer Surprises. Meetings, Incentives Conventions and Exhibitions (the so-called MICE) play a crucial role in enhancing the tourism industry of Dubai and ultimately the UAE economy, attracting some 20% to 30% of the total tourist trade visiting the country (Department of Tourism and Commerce Marketing, 2013).

The main outcome of all the tourism development initiatives is the creation of modern Dubai, a unique cityscape that has attracted a significant number of international visitors (Henderson, 2008; Stephenson & Night, 2010). This dynamic progress and vitality has created an ensemble of rapidly built, large and often distinctively amazing structures, and these have rapidly changed the face of Dubai (Bageen, 2007) to allow it to step with confidence onto the world stage. Modern Dubai is today well positioned on the international tourism map as one of the world's top destinations. However, the Dubai government wishes to expand the sector further. Early in 2013, the ruler of Dubai, His Highness Sheikh Mohammed bin Rashid Al Maktoum, who is widely recognised as the driving force behind the prosperous economic growth and the successful level of tourism development, announced the 'Dubai Tourism Vision 2020' . This vision identifies the goal for Dubai to double its annual visitor arrivals from 10 million in 2012 to 20 million by 2020.

The vision seeks to triple the economic contribution tourism currently makes to the city's economy. If a growth rate in tourist arrivals similar to that attained in 2013 is sustained, this implies a 10.6% year-on -year increase, adding 11 million guests to Dubai if the city-emirate is to achieve its Tourism Vision target. Given that London, with 16 million tourists in 2013, holds the title of 'the world's most visited city', Dubai with its ambitious Tourism Vision 2020 strives to surpass London and be positioned as the single most visited city worldwide. Is that feasible?

Thus, after one year of implementation of the Dubai Tourism Vision 2020, this chapter examines the strategies developed by the emirate's

Tourism Authority to accomplish this vision. Particularly after the Tourism Authority has stated its ambition for Dubai to become 'the world's most visited city', this chapter explores the significant strategies that should be developed to achieve this vision, the strengths and opportunities as well as weaknesses and threats that Dubai must deal with to successfully achieve its bold tourism vision for 2020.

6.2. Literature Review

In spite of the political instability prevailing in most Middle East countries, the average annual growth rate in visitor arrivals in Dubai strives to exceed the global figures (Sharpley, 2008). The city has succeeded in attracting more tourists in 2013 than it did in 2012. The keys to this success are the development of world-class facilities and creative infrastructure projects such as metro Dubai, ring roads, private bridges, double-decked highway flyovers, air-conditioned bus stops, and a monorail system. Dubai International Airport, which has recorded the second highest traffic in the world, plays a significant role in bringing new visitors to Dubai (Bageen, 2007; Stephenson, 2014).

The airport was upgraded to include six new runways and consists of three terminals and has a total capacity of 80 million passengers per year. Terminal 3 is the newest and largest airport terminal in the world and the largest building on earth by floor space. The new upgrading that will make Dubai Airport the world's largest airport, receiving 120 million passengers yearly by 2025, is directed by Sheikh Ahmed bin Rashid Al Maktoum, a member of the royal family and also chairman of the Dubai Civil Aviation and Emirates Airlines (Shapley, 2008). Currently, there are over 7,000 weekly flights operated by 140 airlines to over 230 destinations spread across every continent (Dubai International Airport, 2014).

Moreover, in addition to the major concerts and world-level sporting events, Dubai is leading in the sphere of Meetings Incentives Conferences and Events (MICE) (Sharpley, 2008); this has also played a central role in boosting visitor numbers in the first half of 2013. The Department of Tourism and Commerce Marketing (DTCM) was established in 1997 as the principal tourism authority. This authority, chaired by Dubai's ruler, Shiekh Mohamad bin Rashed AlMaktoum, bears sole responsible for tourism planning, supervision and development (Sharpley, 2008).The DTCM released its tourism figures for the first half of 2013, shown in Table 6.1. Dubai welcomed more than 7.9 million tourists between January and September 2013. As demonstrated in these tables, Dubai achieved a 9.8% cent year-on-year increase in new visitor arrivals.

Moreover, DTCM (2013) figures show increases across all key indicators, including hotel establishment guests, hotel and hotel apartment revenues, room occupancy, and average length of stay. This may indicate that Dubai is indeed on its way to achieving the goals of the Tourism Vision 2020.

Table 6.1 – Dubai's top source markets

January – September 2013			January – September 2012		
Rank	Nationality	Total Guests	Rank	Nationality	Total Guests
1	Saudi Arabia	1,052,353	1	Saudi Arabia	843,568
2	India	631,638	2	India	549,450
3	UK	535,284	3	UK	489,884
4	USA	356,971	4	USA	369,474
5	Russia	263,969	5	Iran	262,881
6	Kuwait	261,346	6	Russia	242,289
7	Germany	234,505	7	Germany	229,685
8	Oman	218,775	8	Kuwait	226,326
9	China	201,036	9	Oman	213,995
10	Iran	196,897	10	China	181,180
11	Australia	194,448	11	Pakistan	178,887
12	Pakistan	185,919	12	Australia	144,121
13	Egypt	152,825	13	France	124,545
14	Qatar	132,435	14	Qatar	123,513
15	France	132,383	15	Egypt	120,307
16	Philippines	95,138	16	Philippines	92,339
17	Italy	90,919	17	Italy	85,942
18	Jordan	85,528	18	Bahrain	76,031
19	Lebanon	80,098	19	Jordan	72,640
20	Bahrain	73,486	20	Lebanon	69,580

Source: Department of Tourism and Commerce Marketing, 2013.

Saudi Arabia and India ranked as the top markets for Dubai for tourists from January to September of 2013, and tourists from UK, U.S., Russia, Germany, Kuwait, Oman, China, and Iran also made it to the list of top 10 nationalities travelling to Dubai for tourism. However, despite the rapid and consistent increase in tourist arrivals in Dubai, some prospective weaknesses can be identified. For example, the average length of stay for hotel guests according to DTCM (2013) figures is just 3.9 days.

Another potential weakness is that the top tourism markets for Dubai are mainly the neighbouring GCC and Middle Eastern countries (Table 6.1), particularly the Kingdom of Saudi Arabia with more than million Saudis visiting Dubai in 2013. Consistently, Saudi Arabia witnessed the highest growth once again, with the number of Saudis visiting Dubai increasing by 24.8% to 1,052,353 (as shown in Table 6.1). However, visitors from Western Europe, particularly the UK, represent the majority of European arrivals, with the UK ranked as the third largest tourism source for Dubai after Saudi Arabia and India. This accounts for an increased share of total arrivals from Western Europe from 20% in 2000 (DTCM, 2006) to 25% in 2013 (DTCM, 2013).

6.3. Methodology

In authoritarian states, significant challenges face researchers regarding collecting primary data and having access to professionals for in-depth interviews (Sharpley, 2008). Nevertheless, the researcher was able to obtain e-mail interviews with tourism planners from the Department of Tourism and Commerce Marketing (DTCM). As mentioned earlier, the DTCM chaired by the ruler of Dubai, was established in 1997 as the principle authority for tourism planning and development. Discussion and findings are based upon analysis of the interview transcripts and the available secondary data, including previous tourism studies, published articles, and tourism figures and reports either published or provided by DTCM through email in addition to fieldwork observations.

6.4. Results

Tourism development in Dubai is under way and has succeeded in placing Dubai in a leading position on the global tourism map. The achievement of its tourism vision of the future will significantly depend on stable and secure circumstances; in a region of uncertainty, these cannot be guaranteed. This continuing development of Dubai implies a growing demand that can keep up with the significant large-scale investment in constructing and expanding the tourism infrastructure and facilities. According to Henderson (2006), Dubai today is at a critical stage: s essential for its development to sustain extraordinary growth, increase length of stay, fill the capacity of the expensive hotels and entertainment facilities and endeavour to create a tourism industry that is economically, socially, and environmentally sustainable.

According to Ross (2001), governments in oil–producing states maintain their authority through a policy of taxation, in this way lowering potential demands for popular representation in the government; in addition, there is extensive spending on a broad range of public projects. Authoritarian rule clearly shapes tourism planning processes in Dubai, with tourism strategies and development formed and decided upon by the state, and high-profile infrastructural development projects are run by the government, in an arrangement that supplants market influences and mechanisms. Moreover, as a result of the centralised planning and development process, the DTCM is in some cases excluded from the overall tourism planning and strategy process, more often being required to react to plans decided upon in meetings at the upper level. For example, according to Sharpley (2008), the official target of attracting 15 million visitors by 2010 was announced by the ruler of Dubai at a press conference, while planners and officials of the DTCM remained uninformed of how that number was arrived at (Sharpley, 2008).

To achieve the Dubai Tourism Vision 2020, the tourism planning authorities should continue with their marketing and product development enterprises to relocate Dubai from simply a luxury destination to a unique vacation spot as well as a distinctive natural and cultural heritage destination. While Dubai's image as a luxury destination is significant for tourism planners and developers in Dubai, official tourism planners of DTCM recognise that they have to show what else Dubai has to offer to the world in order to differentiate their tourism market. Dubai has to plan for mass tourism in order to implement the key aims of the Tourism Vision 2020. Based on the analysis of interview scripts with DTCM officials and the reports and figures provided by them, the following strategies have been identified for Dubai to achieve its ambitious vision.

- Increasing Dubai's 'destination offering' across events, attractions, infrastructure, services and packages and creating and developing more festivals and events.
- Reaching an even wider audience by targeting travellers on a budget and business visitors so that they can consider extending their trip in order to experience Dubai's attractions and activities more fully.
- Maintaining its market share across Dubai's existing source markets as economic and demographic growth will lead to a natural increase in visitors from Dubai's top markets (including Saudi Arabia, the UK, Germany and the U.S.).
- Focusing on tourism markets that have been identified as having high growth potential (such as India, China and Australia).
- Increasing the number of repeat visitors by increased offering of a wider array of experiences.
- Increasing the length of stay of tourists in Dubai which has been identified as a strategic driver of tourism growth within the Tourism Vision 2020.
- Exploiting a network of 22 overseas offices of the DTCM to promote Dubai in almost every main market worldwide while

transforming awareness of the emirate into flight and hotel bookings.

- Conducting a number of broadcasts and market-specific campaigns to position Dubai as a 'destination of choice' to ensure visitors come from a broad range of markets.
- Positioning Dubai as a summer tourism destination, particularly for travellers from the region, by establishing largely indoor attractions to continue attracting visitors in the very hot summer months that tend to keep tourists away. For example, Atlantis is leading a new wave of theme-park style tourist attractions, including Universal Studios, SeaWorld and Legoland. DTCM figures show that the highest levels of hotel guests in 2013 were in the months of January, March, and June respectively, signifying the success of DTCM's strategy.
- Targeting families—a market segment that is growing at six per cent annually in the key Gulf source market—by establishing Dubai as the top family destination. This can be achieved, for example, by offering segmented packages across different themes to ensure that Dubai is perceived as a highly attractive and inviting destination for families. One concrete proposal is to have a 'Kids Go Free' initiative as part of events which offer opportunities for children to stay in hotels and visit tourism attractions at no additional cost.
- Conducting extensive research in order to identify the needs and the expectations of Dubai's top source markets to ensure that the city provides what they need and and want, meeting their expectations, while identifying areas which Dubai can improve upon.
- Unifying the approach to leisure and business tourism, Dubai is already the hub for MICE and trade in the MENASA region (Middle East, North Africa and South Asia). Dubai has the potential to further develop tourism using its existing conference event business infrastructure as a platform for expanding its leisure tourism market. Under the logo 'today's business visitor is tomorrow's leisure tourist', the DTCM is encouraging visitors to extend their length of stay and return for future holidays with families and friends.

In analysing interview manuscripts and the review of the strategies developed by DTCM planners, and based on many academic studies on tourism planning and development in Dubai, SWOT analysis has been conducted (see Table 6.2). The strengths, weaknesses, threats, and opportunities of tourism planning to achieve the Dubai Tourism Vision 2020 have been identified. Barriers must be overcome before opportunities can be fully exploited. Weaknesses and threats that may be addressed include the lack of national planning for tourism development in the UAE; this may result in individual emirates developing their own tourism sector, which implies competition within the UAE itself for a share of similar markets. Moreover, competition from other destinations in the Middle East and the Gulf countries, such as Oman, Qatar, and even Abu Dhabi may further impact on and dilute demand for tourism in Dubai. Furthermore, developed strategies should address the short length of stay and the non-repeat visitors.

On the other hand, non-repeat tourism in Dubai is creating a concern about the continuous rapid development of facilities and attractions; this can result in the supply significantly exceeding the demand. Another significant weakness identified in Dubai tourism planning and development is the dependence of high-profile tourism and infrastructure development projects on regional oil–based capital. Dubai is a 'sink' for enormous profits from oil production in the region (Sharpley, 2008). In 2004, for example, investors from the Kingdom of Saudi Arabia pumped some US$7 billion into key development projects in Dubai (Davis, 2006; Hall, 2005). This continuous dependence on oil-based capital for infrastructural development is not economically sustainable as oil will become scarcer in the region and consequently more expensive, an issue that is evidently recognised by the UAE government. That is reflected in the significant steps undertaken by the Dubai government for economic diversification through tourism.

Table 6.2 – SWOT analysis of tourism planning and development in Dubai

Strengths	Weaknesses
- Strategic location - Political stability - Relatively liberal society - Attractive climate (winter sun) - Impressive desert landscape - High-quality infrastructure and tourism facilities that satisfy modern tastes - Worldwide recognition as a shopping destination - Firmly established on the global retail map	- Relatively short length of stay - Low repeat visitors - Lack of national tourism plan so individual emirates are competing with each other for a share of similar markets. - Centralised planning and development process - Infrastructural development remains dependent on regional oil-based capital

- Economic and tourism policy - Attractions and Events - MICE (Meetings Incentives Conferences and Events) well established	- Rapid modernisation that may create adverse effects on the local society - Tourism planning is centred on high-quality tourist experiences and the needs of the visitor rather than the welfare of those being visited
Opportunities	Threats
- Technology (promoting small and medium-sized tourism agents [TA's] to adopt Internet) - Extensive marketing (with special focus on India and China) - Using its existing conference event business as a platform for expanding its leisure tourism market (capture business visitors to return as leisure tourists) - Economic wealth and investment in world-class facilities - Developing cultural tourism initiatives and the cultural tourism product of the host society. - Winning the right to host EXPO 2020	- Prevailing political instability in the Middle East region - Increased competition from tourism development in other emirates (Abu Dhabi) and other states (Oman and Qatar) - Current global and regional growth rates - Environmental impacts of tourism development and the scarce natural resources(water) - Adverse socio-cultural impacts of tourism development - Continued rapid tourism development may result in supply significantly exceeding demand

On the other hand, social and cultural impacts stemming from tourism are being felt within the UAE (Stephenson, 2014; Stephenson & Ali-Knight, 2010). The marriage of Western schooling and Middle Eastern cultural heritage, while intermixing with a distinctive blend of Indian, European, African, and New World cultures, has created a unique social structure with no mirror images worldwide (Heard-Bey, 2005). Furthermore, Dubai's Westernised and modernised approach to tourism development may be leading to an apparent absence of cultural consistency, particularly in terms of the absorption of the old into the new. Rapid urbanisation and modernisation have had substantial socio-cultural impacts on Islamic tourism destinations in the Middle East. For many reasons, local residents often are the weaker party in interactions with their guests and service providers. The local population in Dubai can be quite ambivalent towards tourism development in their emirate, particularly when the pace of growth is rapid. The environmental and sociocultural threats associated with mass tourism activities should be central in any sustainable tourism planning and development. Tourism planning in Dubai should seek to maximise the economic benefits of tourism and minimise the adverse impacts, while at the same time recognising the 'holistic' nature of tourism – it must plan for the residents and not only for the visitors.

Furthermore, the UAE's foray into tourism development included such studies as environmental impacts, environmental degradation, and environmental carrying capacity (Park & Stephenson, 2007). Park and Stephenson (2007) point out that research showed a significantly large environmental capacity was possible in the UAE, thus resulting in the mass tourism concept Dubai chose to pursue. As more has been learned in recent decades about the volatile nature of the sociocultural effects of tourism, and as societal functions lessen the amount of impacts deemed acceptable, there is a need to revisit policies. To date, however, repeat visits continue to focus solely on environmental concerns; there is a need to recognise the sociocultural influences of tourism (Park & Stephenson, 2007).

Negative impacts may include increased cultural conflict and changes in the vernacular landscape in Dubai. Tourism also may lead to higher prices for goods and services, higher cost for real estate and land, traffic congestion and noise pollution. However, planners in the city recognise that cultural products should be developed within the hospitality and tourism industry that represent the true culture of the local population in Dubai. This is not only because of the significance of developing cultural products as resources for international leisure tourists to appreciate and through which they learn about the distinctive host society of Dubai, but also because these products are culturally important for the national population.

On the other hand, many opportunities are identified that Dubai can fully exploit to achieve its Tourism Vision 2020. For example, a list of all certified small and medium–sized tourism agents in Dubai was provided to the researcher by the DTCM;, it was noticed that many of them do not have websites or do not adopt Internet technology in their business. Adoption of Internet and e–commerce technology by small and medium-sized travel agencies presents opportunities for these companies, which are the backbone of the tourism sector, to employ the benefits of ICTs in reaching new customers and suppliers (Abou Al Shouk *et al.*, 2013; Kim, 2005). Internet adoption is the best marketing tool for travel agencies in Dubai and a device for their competitive advantage.

Benefits resulting from using technology include designing and delivering new products, direct access to new markets, and increasing productivity (Poon, 1993). Developing online booking systems and effective websites also could attract new customers and assist in the retention of current customers (Abou Al Shouk *et al.*, 2013). Thus, it is suggested that encouraging travel agencies in Dubai to adopt e-commerce could represent an opportunity to expand the tourism market, which is a step toward achieving the Dubai Tourism Vision 2020. Furthermore, the MICE tourists should be considered as a 'captive audience', since it will be easier for tourism planners to develop extra packages for existing tourists who are visiting Dubai for business purposes rather than attracting potential tourists who may not be considering the Middle East region as a leisure destination (Sharpley, 2008). Business travellers, if promoted with additional packages to explore Dubai, are more likely to consider returning to the emirate with their families and friends for leisure purposes.

Moreover, tourism planners should benefit from the increasing propensity for people from China and India to travel overseas by aiming at maintaining growth of these high-potential markets (as shown in Table 1). This growth may be maintained by opening more offices of the DTCM in these countries to further expand the marketing and promotional activities. One more action that may be considered by tourism policymakers is establishing a partnership between Emirates Airlines and Indian and Chinese airlines to improve the accessibility between Dubai and these countries.

Finally, with shopping emerging recently as the most preferred tourism activity and a determining factor in destination selection, Dubai has significant competitive advantages as a shopping destination. Thios includes high-quality shopping venues, ranging from Dubai luxury shopping malls to the traditional Arab souks, a wide variety of products, significant shopping promotions and bargains, annual shopping festivals such as the Dubai Shopping Festival and Dubai Summer Surprises, and most importantly, the creativity in combining shopping experiences with a cluster of entertainment and leisure opportunities.

Every mall in Dubai has developed its own way to combine the shopping experience with an ensemble of unique options for entertainment and leisure. Footfalls at malls in Dubai range between 20 million at Dierah Mall (Dierah Mall, 2014) to 75 million each year at Dubai Mall (Dubai Mall, 2014), which made this mall the world's most-visited destination for three years successively. Accordingly, the Dubai government should proceed with marketing and product development initiatives to further the position of Dubai as a global vacation destination and a shopping haven, particularly for more than one million Saudis visiting Dubai each year. Saudi tourists are the top source tourism market for Dubai, and maintaining this market is one of the strategies that should be developed in order to achieve its Tourism Vision 2020.

6.5. Conclusion

Tourism development in Dubai is driven by a significant target of 20 million visitors by 2020, requiring arrivals to more than double in six years. Achieving Dubai Tourism Vision also entails an annual growth of nine per cent, which is in line with current growth rates, according to the data released by the DTCM. Economic wealth and investment in expensive facilities have successfully generated strong economic growth in tourism. Dubai is a hub between East and West and is a natural gateway to emerging tourism markets. Apparently, all key factors in order for Dubai to achieve its Tourism Vision 2020 already exist, particularly after Dubai won the bidding for hosting EXPO 2020. For a period of six months, this EXPO will attract millions of visitors. Indeed, Dubai may celebrate all its development achievements, yet the feasibility of achieving its ambition to be the world top tourism destination may be debatable.

As discussed earlier, Dubai still has to overcome many barriers to its development as a destination and to achieve its tourism vision. Furthermore, despite Dubai's optimistic tourism development enterprises and the distinctive expansion of its tourism facilities and infrastructure over the past twenty years, the initial concern is what strategies should be developed by the tourism planning authorities in Dubai not only to achieve the determined target of attracting 20 million visitors by 2020 but also to endorse a sustainable long-term tourist growth.

Destination marketing objectives that extensively focus on re-positioning Dubai from a luxury and exclusive destination to a more attainable and cost-attractive destination are crucial. Given the global downturn which affects the economic capacities of tourists originating from Dubai's top source markets such as the U.S., the UK, Germany, and Russia, in addition to the tourism industry's economic requirements to sustain the modernisation of Dubai and the rapid development of tourist-serving infrastructure and facilities (such as hotels, amusement parks, malls, and event and leisure destinations), the prospect of developing budget hotels in Dubai is significantly encouraging. Establishing or expanding budget hotels has not conventionally been of high importance for local and foreign investors, since developers preferred luxury hotels because of the high land prices and investment costs.

Moreover, shopping is a desired tourism activity for most tourists visiting Dubai. Tourism planners and developers should consider building new shopping venues in other developing areas of Dubai. Shopping-festival tourism has proven to be successful in offering exciting opportunities for tourists and enriching their shopping experience. Dubai's strength lies in its stable government that has proved to be an innovator and a leader in creating the most modern tourist destination and most favoured shopping heaven in one of the most unstable regions of the world.

The state-of-the-art shopping venues and contemporary malls with appealing entertainment and leisure areas have been successful in attracting increasing number of tourists each year who are seeking luxury products and services. Accordingly, policy-makers should consider exerting greater efforts in designing the right marketing mix to attract shoppers and to inform them of the advantages of participating in the distinctive and superb shopping experiences in Dubai. Environmentally and culturally, it is strongly suggested that future research should be conducted to examine the perceptions and attitudes of residents regarding the sociocultural impacts of tourism.

The host population and their attitude toward the presence of tourists in their city are likely to be important planning and policy considerations for successful tourism development, marketing, and operation of existing and future programs and projects. Likewise, more attempts should be made to embrace environmental objectives in tourism planning and development in Dubai. Moreover, more research should be conducted in order to assess the environmental impacts of attracting increasing numbers of tourists to Dubai.

Although tourism planning and development in Dubai is characterised by authoritarian central control, the political economy of Dubai and the ability of the Dubai government to invest both financially and politically in high-profile infrastructural tourism projects have certainly reinforced the outstanding achievements of tourism development in the emirate. Yet, tourism policy and planning in Dubai follows a hyper-model that is a combination of authoritarian central control and positive features of contemporary planning models in developed market-led economies as public-private partnerships.

In sum, Dubai's emergence as a tourist destination is an outcome of prevailing specific political, economic and sociocultural conditions. Consequently, accomplishing the 'Dubai Tourism Vision 2020' will certainly face many challenges and barriers that the city can best overcome by developing sustainable strategies for tourism planning and development. The question that may rise in this process is whether the Dubai Tourism Vision 2020 is even desirable, given the probable adverse social, cultural and environmental impacts, which could potentially constitute further obstacles to sustainable long-term tourist growth.

Acknowledgement

The author would like to thank Dr. Mark Andrew Scott, University of United Arab Emirates (UAEU), for his review and constructive comments that assisted me in revising this chapter.

References

Abou-Shouk, M., Lim, W.M., & Megicks, P. (2013). Internet adoption by travel agents: A case of Egypt. *International Journal of Tourism Research,* 15. 298–312

AME Info (2006). Dubailand to double Dubai hotel rooms, AME Info Middle East. Available at www.ameinfo.-com/84720.html [accessed 27 June 2014]

Bageen, S. (2007). Brand Dubai: The instant city; or the instantly city recognized city. *International Planning Studies*, 12(2), 173-197.

Davis, M. 2006. Fear and money in Dubai. *New Left Review*, 41, 47–68.

Deirah City Center (2014). 'Home': about us. http://www.deiracitycentre.com/about-us.aspx [accessed 28 June 2014].

Department of Tourism and Commerce Marketing (2006). *Dubai visitor survey 2002–2003*. Dubai: Department of Tourism and Commerce Marketing.

Department of Tourism and Commerce Marketing (2013). Dubai welcomes over 7.9 million visitors in first nine months of 2013. Available at http://chfr.dubaixperts.com/index.php?option=com_ content&view=article&id=741%3Adubai-welcomes-over-79-million-visitors-in-first-nine-months-of-2013&catid=1%3Alatest-news [accessed 6 March 2013].

Dubai International Airport (2014). http://www.dubaiairport.com [accessed 2 March 2014].

Dubai Mall (2014). http://www.thedubaimall.com/en/Index.aspx. [accessed 8 July 2014].

Economic Intelligence Unit (EIU). (2003). *UAE country report*, April 2003, available at http://search.proquest.com/docview/ 466357372? accountid=62373 [accessed 5 July 2014].

Hall, C.M. (2005). The role of government in the management of tourism. In L. Pender & R. Sharpley (eds.). *The management of tourism* (pp. 217–231). London: Sage.

Heard-Bey, F. (2005). The United Arab Emirates: Statehood and nation-building in a traditional society. *The Middle East Journal*, 59(3), 357–375.

Henderson, J.C. (2008). Tourism in Dubai: Overcoming barriers to destination development. *International Journal of Tourism Research.* 8, 87-99.

—. (2007). Destination development. *Journal of Travel & Tourism Marketing*, 20(3-4), 33-45.

Khaleej Times (2013). Dubai builds, tourists come. Available at http://www.khaleejtimes.com/kt-article-display-1.asp?xfile=data/nationgeneral/2013/August/nationgeneral_August212.xml&section=nationgeneral [accessed 3 March 2013].

Kim C. (2005). Enhancing the role of tourism SMEs in global value chain: a case analysis on travel agencies and tour operators in Korea. Global tourism growth: a challenge for SMEs. Available at http://www.oecd.org/dataoecd/26/48/36886129.pdf [accessed 8 June 2015].

Park, H.Y., & Stephenson, M.L. (2007). A critical analysis of the symbolic significance of heritage tourism. *International Journal of Excellence in Tourism, Hospitality and Catering*, 1(2), 34–60.

Poon, A. (1993). *Tourism, technology and competitive strategies.* Oxon: CABI.

Ross, M. (2001). Does oil hinder democracy? *World Politics*, 51(3), 325–361.

Sharply, R. (2008). Planning for tourism: The case of Dubai. *Tourism and Hospitality Planning & Development*, 5(1), 13-30.

Smith, B. (2010). Scared by, of, in, and for Dubai. *Social & Cultural Geography*, 11(3), 263-283.

Stephenson, M. (2014). Tourism, development and 'destination Dubai': Cultural dilemmas and future challenges. *Current Issues in Tourism.* 17(8), 723-738. Stephenson, M., & Night, J. (2010). Dubai's tourism industry and its societal impact: social implications and sustainable challenges. *Journal of Tourism and Cultural Change*, 8(4), 278-292.

CHAPTER SEVEN

THE INFLUENCE OF HUMAN–ENVIRONMENT
INTERACTION ON ADVENTURE TOURISM

JULIA K. GIDDY

Abstract

Despite the consensus that the environment plays an important role in adventure tourism (AT), the strength of the environment in attracting participation in AT has yet to be adequately investigated. This chapter seeks to explore this research opportunity by re-examining both sides of the human-environment relationship within the AT context. Particular attention is given to the attractive force of the environment amongst participants in five different adventure activities in the Tsitsikamma region of South Africa. The findings show the relative strength of environmental influences on AT motivations and experiences as well as participants' perceptions of environmental impact in the context of these activities. They demonstrate that the environment plays an important but varying role in AT motivations and experiences while perceptions of environmental impact are relatively low and homogenous. **Keywords:** adventure tourism, human-environment interaction, motivations, environmental impact.

7.1. Introduction

Adventure tourism (AT) is one of the fastest growing sectors of the tourism industry. Hall (1992, p.143) defines AT as "a broad spectrum of outdoor touristic activities, often commercialised and involving an interaction with the natural environment away from the participants' home range and containing elements of risk" (Hall, 1992, p.143). It is also considered part of the broad spectrum of alternative tourism, namely, nature-based and ecotourism, known as NEAT tourism (Buckley, 2000). While AT used to be limited to a small number of elite, highly skilled and physically fit participants (Varley, 2006), an increased demand for new and unique experiences has evolved. A wide range of activities is now offered to eager participants who have little to no skills and sometimes even low levels of physical fitness (Buckley, 2007). This development of commercial AT has changed the industry substantially (Beedie & Hudson, 2003; Williams & Soutar, 2005). It has also created the need to re-evaluate early perceptions of, and assumptions about, AT (Pomfret, 2011).

The growing awareness concerning environmental matters, particularly the mitigation of environmental impacts, has led to a need to better understand the relationship between humans and the environment (Luo & Deng, 2007). This approach can apply to every aspect of life, but is particularly interesting when considered in terms of direct human interactions with nature. While much discussion, in terms of this relationship in AT, focuses on the physical environmental impacts caused by humans (Buckley, 2004, 2010; Fennell, 2008), little attention has been given to the influence the environment itself has on human perceptions and behaviour. AT provides an ideal context for readdressing this imbalance. The aim of this study is, therefore, to clarify the influence of human-environment interaction in the context of nature-based AT, by assessing not only human influences on the environment, but importantly environmental influences on humans. This is done by analysing the perceptions of participants in five different commercial AT activities in a single destination, the Tsitsikamma, South Africa.

7.2. Literature Review

Apart from general works that have reviewed the AT industry as a whole (Buckley, 2006, 2007, 2010; Rogerson, 2007; Swarbrooke, Beard, Leckie, & Pomfret, 2003), more detailed research has focused on two aspects. The first stresses the physical environmental impacts of specific AT activities, (Buckley, Weaver, & Pickering, 2001; Buckley, 2004, 2010) and the second the motivations for participation in AT which have stressed risk-seeking behaviour, (Cater, 2006; Ewert & Hollenhorst, 1989; Robinson, 1992). These thems will briefly be elaborated upon below.

7.2.1. Environmental impacts

AT and ecotourism tend to take place in unique, remote and often fragile environments (Buckley, 2004). This is partially due to the landscape requirements of these types of tourism but also to meet the need to validate experiences within a unique setting (Bell & Lyall, 2002). With the growth of so-called "green" initiatives and increasing awareness of larger environmental impacts in recent years, there has been a great deal of research that examines the physical environmental impacts caused by AT activities (Buckley, 2004; Camp & Knight, 1998; Farris, 1998; Fennell, 2008). Furthermore, although participants are not often able to identify specific impacts, two important findings emerge. First, perceptions of impact in comparison with actual environmental impact assessments, have found that there seems to be a degree of impact that is considered acceptable (Manning *et al.,* 2008). Second, participants tended to give lower ratings to sites with higher environmental impacts. This means that visitor perceptions are important (Hillery, Nancarrow, Syme, & Land, 2001). On the one hand, they demonstrate the aspects of environmental impact of which visitors are aware. On the other, they are possibly a more effective means of encouraging operators to take note of and effectively manage environmental impacts that could directly influence visitor satisfaction with environmental quality.

The essential role that the environment plays in the AT industry has been stressed (Pomfret, 2006, 2012; Swarbrooke *et al.*, 2003; Williams & Soutar, 2005). Yet, environmental protection is not a priority in many AT operations making it one of the critical issues facing the industry (Williams & Soutar, 2005). The lack of regulation within the industry, coupled with the rapid increase in the emergence of AT operations, has led to an increase in environmental degradation. Ironically, this leads to a decrease in the attractiveness of said environment (Williams & Soutar, 2005). Therefore it is pertinent for the survival of the industry that operators carefully consider the impacts of their operations on the environment and take steps to minimise and manage the damaged caused by such activities.

7.2.2. Adventure tourist motivations and perceptions linked to the environment

Studies have found that there is a relationship between different types of NEAT tourism and environmental awareness (Brymer, 2009; Kim, Borges, & Chon, 2006; Luo & Deng, 2007). Of these, two studies have examined the relationship between environmental values and motivations. The first, a study by Luo and Deng (2007) of visitors to a Chinese national park, found that participants with higher environmental values were more likely to be motivated by the ability to "return to nature" (p.399). Another by Kim, Borges and Chon (2006) on attendees to an environmental film festival in Brazil, found that those with higher environmental values were in fact more likely to be motivated by environmental aspects. Several studies have also found evidence that frequent practitioners of risky sports are more likely to have eco–centric attitudes, arguing that repeat participation in such sports can increase environmental awareness by developing a renewed respect for nature (Brymer & Gray, 2010; Brymer, 2009).

A 'push' and 'pull' factor approach to tourism motivations can also be observed. First applied to tourism by Dann (1977), this approach is based on the concept that there are certain internal aspects that *push* an individual to seek out specific tourism opportunities and the choice of which product/destination to choose is dependent on external *pull* factors unique to that particular experience. The combination of these two elements leads to an individual's decision to choose that specific experience. This approach has been effectively applied to numerous tourism studies (Crompton, 1979; Kim, Lee, & Klenosky, 2003; Uysal & Jurowski, 1994) including AT, specifically, most notably by Pomfret (2006) in the context of mountaineering tourism. Pomfret (2006, p.117) lists catharsis, physical setting, recognition and challenge as examples of 'push' factors, while 'pull' factors focus primarily on specific aspects of the mountain environment. The combination of these internal and external factors, as perceived by the individual, leads to the development of a personal perception of adventure and subsequently the decision of whether to engage (i.e. participate in the activity) or to withdraw.

The vast majority of research pertaining to tourism motivations has focused on 'push' factors (Kim, Lee, & Klenosky, 2003). This is particularly true in AT motivations where literature concentrates largely on notions of risk or thrill. Early studies found that actual physical risk was the primary motivation for adventure recreation, using evidence of risk-seeking personality traits (Ewert & Hollenhorst, 1989; Robinson, 1992). Recent studies, however, have found that inciting feelings of thrill, fear or "rush" rather than actual physical risk is a more accurate assessment of motivations participants in today's AT industry which has become largely commercialised (Buckley, 2012; Cater, 2006). In this context, participants seek thrilling experiences with the absence of actual risk. Others, still, have argued that all notions of risk or thrill are just secondary (Kane & Tucker, 2004; Walle, 1997).

Perceptions of tourists have been analysed at length by Urry and Larsen (2011). In the context of AT, they contextualise the notion of the tourist gaze by arguing that landscape is at the core of human experiences with nature. Furthermore, Bell and Lyall (2002) emphasise the role the setting of a particular activity has on validation and social value. They argue that an activity is only valued if it occurs in a unique and exciting location (Bell & Lyall, 2002). Williams and Soutar (2009) found that social value is an important factor in participants' choice of a tourism product. Increases in technology and particularly social media further this, by allowing participants to proudly display their conquests for the world, increasing their social value and creating their accelerated "adventure" identity (Bell & Lyall, 2002; Kane & Tucker, 2004).

7.2.3. Conceptual framework

A theoretical framework designed to elucidate tourist motivations associated with the landscape requires at least two characteristics. The first would be an overarching explanation of human-environment interaction, and the second, an account of how such motivations could operate. To meet these requirements, this study adapted the framework developed by Constantino, Falcitelli, Femia, and Tuolini (2003). This was then further modified to incorporate Pomfret's (2006) specific view of tourist motivations which included both 'push' and 'pull' factors (Figure 7.1).

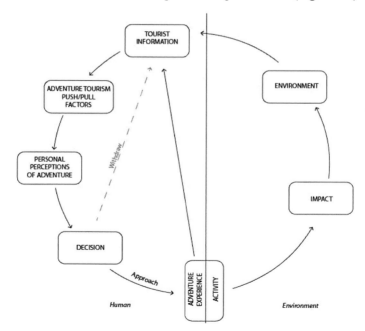

Figure 7.1 – A framework for human-environment interaction

A consideration of the above framework indicates that a participant in AT would first gather initial 'information' on the place, activity and the environment concerned. This 'information' is then filtered through the individual's value system comprised (in this context) of 'push' and 'pull' factors. 'Push' factors are internal motivation factors that drive people toward specific tourism experiences while 'pull' factors are external aspects of the particular activity or destination that draw people towards that specific experience. The resulting 'perception' then leads to 'decision' to participate. The effect of participation on the environment is an 'impact', that to varying degrees, alters the 'environment' and therefore how it is perceived in the future.

7.3. Methodology

The research was conducted using participants in five different AT activities in the Tsitsikamma region of the Eastern Cape province of South Africa. This area was chosen because of its unique and striking landscape, its location along the popular South African Garden Route and the wide range of activities available. This particular region has played a large role in the recent rebranding of the Eastern Cape as the "Adventure Province" (Eastern Cape Tourism Board, 2009). More specifically, the study seeks to examine the differences in motivations and experiences *within* the AT industry by assessing participant perceptions over a range of AT activities. Activities that were used vary in terms of price, duration, group size, setting and levels of physical fitness required. Similar activities with a slightly different setting and run by different operators are also utilised in order to examine the different dynamics relating to setting and operator. The following five activities were chosen: bungee jumping (BJ); canopy tours (CT); ziplining (ZP); and two black-water tubing activities (BT1 & BT2).

Questionnaires, distributed to participants in select activities in the Tsitsikamma were the primary data source. Questions were limited to fixed response answers due to the need for brevity when collecting data from tourists. The questionnaires focused on the motivations, experiences and perceptions of environmental impact, and were assessed using a 'push' and 'pull' factor approach, see Pomfret's (2006) and Sung, Morrison & O'Leary (1996). The researcher chose 'pull' factors that relate specifically to the Tsitsikamma, derived from landscape qualities outlined in Tviet, Ode & Fry's (2006) framework for landscape analysis. The integrated experiences of participants, related to the motivation factors, were also elicited in order to demonstrate the changes in perceptions from motivations to experiences. Nearly all options for influential aspects of the experience were identical to motivation ('push') factors with the exception of 'novelty,' which was removed due to the fact that the activity is no longer novel. It was replaced with 'emotional experiences' alluding to numerous discussions in research of "flow," often associated with AT (Pomfret, 2012; Wu & Liang, 2011). A total of 405 questionnaires were used and analysed using basic, descriptive statistics. The data is discussed first as whole and then disaggregated into specific activities. The purpose of this is to determine whether or not is appropriate to generalise perceptions of AT participants across a range of activities.

Interviews were also conducted with one owner or manager of each tourism operation used in this study. The purpose of interviews was twofold. The first was to gain insight into the perceptions of the operators in terms of the importance of the environment in attracting tourists their specific activity. The second was to gauge the level of responsibility that they felt towards the environment in which their activity took place. As a result of the interviews, ratings were given to each operation in terms of environmental initiatives. A total of five interviews were conducted, and were transcribed and coded to extract themes related to the above initiatives.

7.4. Results

The findings that emerge from this investigation can be categorised into two sections, namely, human influences on the environment and environmental influences on AT. The first section is linked to initiatives taken by tourist operators as well as the perceptions of those participating in the AT activities. The second, on the other hand, focuses on motivations for participating in an AT activity and the specific aspects of the environment that were found to be particularly attractive and influential. The relative importance of the environment as it relates to both impacts and motivations is also assessed.

7.4.1. Human influences on the environment

The ratings that were given to each operator were broken down into four categories: environmental philosophy, environmental education, environmental mitigations and environmental responsibility. A rating was given, from one to three, for each category. The results were then totaled to give each operator an overall rating out of a possible twelve. The operator of the CT had the highest rating, while the BJ operator had the lowest. The former operator not only places a strong emphasis on the importance of environmental protection but applied these by continuously developing environmentally-friendly facilities. The BJ operator, in contrast, appeared to do the bare minimum and did not profess any need to increase initiatives. The companies that run BT1 and BT2 both rated highly in the environmental mitigation category and moderately in terms of philosophy and responsibility, but environmental education was lacking for all activities. The ZP seemed to have a sense of environmental responsibility and philosophy but only marginally put this into practice (Table 7.1).

Table 7.1 – Human influences on the environment

		Percentage Response					
		BJ	CT	ZP	BT1	BT2	Total
Perceptions of Impact	No Impact	29	18	10	16	12	20
	Little Impact	39	58	47	58	76	49
	Some Impact	23	19	32	21	12	23
	Strong Impact	9	5	11	5	0	8
Changes in Environmental Awareness	Yes	16	48	27	26	12	27
	No	84	52	73	74	88	73
		BJ	**CT**	**ZP**	**BT1**	**BT2**	
Operator Initiatives Rating	Environmental Philosophy	1	3	2	3	2	
	Environmental Education	1	3	1	1	1	
	Environmental Mitigations	1	3	1	3	3	
	Environmental Responsibility	2	3	2	2	2	
Total		5	12	6	9	8	

Participants were then asked their perceptions of environmental impact caused by the activities. The results show that the majority of participants felt that the activity had little to no impact on the environment (Table 7.1). The results also show that participants in activities where operators have stronger environmental initiatives do not necessarily perceive less of an impact than operators with little to no environmental concern or behaviour. This is particularly clear when comparing the results from the operator with the highest rating for environmental initiatives, CT, with that with the lowest, BJ. Although the BJ operator took very few environmental initiatives, BJ participants were the most likely to state that the activity had no impact on the environment. Furthermore, although the CT operator adopted a relatively strong stance on environmental issues which are evident throughout participation and demonstrated in practice, particularly when compared to a relatively similar activity ZP, there was not significant discrepancy in participants' perceptions. These results, therefore, indicate that although operators vary significantly in initiatives taken to ensure environmental protection, participants do not necessarily perceive these differences. Participants were also asked whether or not they felt their environmental awareness was changed as a result of activity participation. The majority of participants, generally, did not feel that their environmental awareness was changed as a result of activity participation. However, the results from the CT had the highest percentage of participants (49%) who did, in fact, feel that their awareness changed as a result of activity participation and only slightly fewer than those who felt that their awareness did not changed (51%). This implies that the environmental initiatives taken by an operator can, potentially, impact the possibility of increased environmental awareness as a result of activity participation.

7.4.2. Environmental influences on adventure tourism

Results relating to 'pull' factors, aspects of the natural environment that attracted participants to the area, included specific features of the environment and landscape qualities. Important features were forests, gorges/canyons, and mountains, features that were reasonably distributed across the various activities. The exception is seen in the CT results, with the vast majority (70%) attracted by forests. Attractive landscape qualities were also quite varied, though qualities that visitors found particularly attractive were the grandeur of the landscape and the uniqueness of the environment, also fairly consistent between participants in different activities. These results show that a range of both landscape features and qualities attracted or pulled participants towards the Tsitsikamma.

The 'push' factors focused on motivations for activity participation. The results found that although 'risk/thrill' featured quite strongly in AT motivations, 'novelty' of the activity and the 'attractiveness of the environment' were also significant, Table 7.2. When the results are distributed by activity, other interesting findings arise. Firstly, 'risk/thrill' is only the top motivating factor for two of the five activities. The two activities for which this was the case, BJ and ZP, entail high levels of adventure and are clearly marketed primarily as high-level adventure activities. Interestingly, both BT1 and BT2 participants found the 'attractiveness of the environment' to be the most important motivation factor, though BT2 participants were as often motivated by 'novelty.' Participants in the CT were most often motivated by 'novelty' but were also likely to be influenced by the 'attractiveness of the environment.'

Table 7.2 – Human motivation and experience factors

		Percentage Response					
		BJ	CT	ZP	BT1	BT2	Total
Motivations	*Physical challenge*	14	13	16	16	6	14
	Attractiveness of the environment	7	33	17	42	35	20
	Impression given by company/organization	1	1	1	5	12	2
	Environmental education	3	2	3	0	0	3
	Risk/Thrill	57	15	43	16	12	37
	Novelty of the activity	18	36	20	21	35	24
Experiences	*Physical challenge*	15	12	17	10	5	14
	Attractiveness of the environment	4	44	39	55	85	32
	Organization of the activity	1	3	6	0	0	3
	Environmental education	0	6	2	0	0	2
	Risk/Thrill	69	27	30	25	5	42
	Emotional experiences	11	8	6	10	5	7

These above results demonstrate a wide variety of AT motivations. No one factor clearly emerged as the most significant, both across the range of activities and often even within a single activity (with the exception of BJ participants). Thus, these findings question the validity of generalising AT motivations which seems to occur in other studies, see Beedie & Hudson (2003); Holyfield (1999); Williams & Soutar, (2009). However, the two exceptions were 'environmental education' and the 'influence of the companies' on participant motivations - two factors that were insignificant across the entire range of activities. The former is particularly interesting in relation to the discussion of ecotourism versus AT. 'Environmental education,' by definition, is an important element of ecotourism, but seemingly not important in AT.

The changes in the perceptions of 'push' and 'pull' factors varied. As far as the 'pull' factors are concerned, these proved relatively insignificant especially when landscape qualities were analysed. The most significant changes are seen in the results pertaining to 'push' or human motivation factors for activity participation. Interestingly, the environment seems to play a slightly more significant role in the integrated experiences of participants than in motivations. Participants in all activities but one most frequently felt that the 'attractiveness of the environment' was the most significant aspect of the experience though with varying degrees. The one exception was the BJ activity, in which the vast majority of participants felt that 'risk/thrill' was the most influencing aspect of their experience, a 12% increase from motivations. There was a significant increase in those influenced by the environment from the ZP (22%) and BT2 (50%). From these results, it is evident that participation in the activity can affect perceptions of influential factors. This could, in turn, alter perceptions of similar activities in the future, changing what is called 'tourist information.' Furthermore, the findings once again, bring to light the issue of generalising AT across the spectrum of activities.

7.5. Conclusion

Perceptions of impact were homogenous across the range of activities despite the fact that certain operators have stronger environmental initiatives. This implies that the environmental initiatives taken by operators do not seem to have a significant effect on participant perceptions of impact in support of previous research that a certain level of impact is tolerated by tourists (Manning *et al.*, 2008). One possible solution to this is for companies with strong environmental initiatives to not only highlight more clearly these initiatives but also to possibly demonstrate the consequences of disregarding the environment. Increasing environmental education before and during the activity is one potential means of achieving this goal. Furthermore, it could potentially encourage participants to support environmentally-conscious operations in the future. The results also found that although operators with stronger environmental initiatives have a slightly higher potential to change environmental awareness, the majority of participants did not experience change.

The findings show that participants found a wide range of 'pull' factors, related to the environment, important. The strength of features such as mountains and canyons/gorges as well as landscape qualities such as grandeur of the landscape, demonstrate that participants found extreme features particularly attractive. When considering human motivation factors and influential aspects of the experience, the results demonstrate that although 'risk/thrill' plays an important role in AT motivations and experiences, it is not the only influencing factor. According to these results, 'risk/thrill' is only one possible motivation for participation and only in the most extreme activities. 'Novelty' and the environment also prove significant. Interestingly, the environment seems to play a slightly more significant role in the integrated experiences of participants than in motivations. The differences in motivations and experiences of participants in different activities refute the notion that they can be generalised. The nature of the activity seems to influence motivations and experience significantly. Furthermore, although *primary* motivation factors and influential aspects of the experience for AT should not be generalised, 'environmental education' and the 'influence of the company' appear to be unimportant across the range of activities.

In discussing the links between human influences and environmental influence some interesting trends emerge. According to the results outlined above, perceptions of the influence of the environment on humans are stronger than that of humans on the environment. The results show that participants feel that the environment, generally, has quite a strong influence on AT motivations and experiences. Some research has touched upon this concept by highlighting the importance of the environment in the experience (Bell & Lyall, 2002; Pomfret, 2006, 2012), but much work remains to be done on this aspect. Furthermore, the influence of the environment on the individual in the AT context is extremely dynamic, with significant variation between activities and between different individuals. This is particularly evident when compared with the information gathered on participant perceptions of the influence of humans on the environment which is somewhat generic –a interesting finding when seen in the context of much previous research which has focused so heavily on the impact of tourists on the environment (Buckley, 2004; Fennell, 2008).

The purpose of this study was to demonstrate the importance of the physical environment and setting in nature-based AT because such activities take place in unique, often remote and fragile ecosystems (Buckley, 2010; Hall, 1992; Williams & Soutar, 2005). The hope is that it will encourage tourism operators, participants and regulators to consider not only effects of AT on the environment, but also increase awareness of the influence the attractiveness of the environment has on AT participation. Continued research is needed to further understand the many environmental perspectives in AT in different contexts. Furthermore, the researcher encourages communication and engagement with stakeholders, particularly tourism operators and institutions in order to utilise the findings and put theory into practice.

References

Beedie, P., & Hudson, S. (2003). Emergence of mountain-based adventure tourism. *Annals of Tourism Research*, 30(3), 625–643.

Bell, C., & Lyall, J. (2002). The accelerated sublime: Thrill-seeking adventure heroes in the commodified landscape. In *Tourism: between place and performance* (pp.21–37). New York: Berghahn Books.

Brymer, E. (2009). Extreme sports as a facilitator of ecocentricity and positive life changes. *World Leisure Journal*, 51(1), 47–53.

Brymer, E., & Gray, T. (2010). Developing an intimate "relationship" with nature through extreme sports participation. *Leisure/Loisir*, 34(4), 361–374.

Buckley, R. (2000). NEAT trends: current issues in nature, eco- and adventure tourism. *International Journal of Tourism Research*, 2(6), 437–444.

Buckley, R. (ed., 2004). *Environmental Impact of Ecotourism*. Cambridge: CABI.

Buckley, R. (2006). *Adventure Tourism*. Cambridge: CABI.

—. (2007). Adventure tourism products: Price, duration, size, skill, remoteness. *Tourism Management*, 28(6), 1428–1433.

—. (2010). *Adventure Tourism Management*. Amsterdam: Butterworth-Heinemann.

—. (2012). Rush as a key motivation in skilled adventure tourism: Resolving the risk recreation paradox. *Tourism Management*, 33(4), 961–970.

Buckley, R., Weaver, D., & Pickering, C. (2001). *Nature-based tourism, environment and land management*. Cambridge: CABI.

Camp, R., & Knight, R. (1998). Effects of rock climbing on cliff plant communities at Joshua Tree National Park, California. *Conservation Biology*, 12(6), 1302–1306.

Cater, C.I. (2006). Playing with risk? participant perceptions of risk and management implications in adventure tourism. *Tourism Management*, 27(2), 317–325.

Constantino, C., Falcitelli, F., Femia, A., & Tuolini, A. (2003). Human-environment interaction. ISTAT, OECD-Workshop, Paris, May 14 -16 2003.

Crompton, J.L. (1979). Motivations for pleasure vacations. *Annals of Tourism Research*, 6(4), 408–424.

Dann, G. (1977). Anomie, ego-enhancement and tourism. *Annals of Tourism Research*, 4(4), 184–194.

Eastern Cape Tourism Board (2009). Eastern Cape tourism board; accommodation, tourism, travel, information. Retrieved January 15, 2014, from http://www.ectourism.co.za/

Ewert, A., & Hollenhorst, S.J. (1989). Testing the adventure model: Empirical support for a model of risk recreation participation. *Journal of Leisure Research*, 21(2), 124.

Farris, M. (1998). The effects of rock climbing on the vegetation of three Minnesota cliff systems. *Canadian Journal of Botony*, 76, 1981–1990.

Fennell, D. (2008). *Ecotourism* (3rd ed.). London: Routledge.

Hall, C. (1992). Adventure, sport and health tourism. In C.M. Hall & B. Weiler (eds.), *Special interest tourism*. London: Belhaven Press.

Hillery, M., Nancarrow, B., Syme, G., & Land, C. (2001). Tourist perception of environmental impact. *Annals of Tourism Research,* 28(4), 853–867.

Holyfield, L. (1999). Manufacturing adventure: The buying and selling of emotions. *Journal of Contemporary Ethnography*, 28(1), 3–32.

Kane, M.J., & Tucker, H. (2004). Adventure tourism: The freedom to play with reality. *Tourist Studies*, 4(3), 217–234.

Kim, H., Borges, M.C., & Chon, J. (2006). Impacts of environmental values on tourism motivation: The case of FICA, Brazil. *Tourism Management*, 27(5), 957–967.

Kim, S.S., Lee, C.-K., & Klenosky, D.B. (2003). The influence of push and pull factors at Korean national parks. *Tourism Management*, 24(2), 169–180.

Luo, Y., & Deng, J. (2007). The new environmental paradigm and nature-based tourism motivation. *Journal of Travel Research*, 46(4), 392–402.

Manning, R., Lawson, S., Newman, P., Budruk, M., Valliere, W., Laven, D., & Bacon, J. (2008). Visitor perceptions of recreation-related resource impacts. In R. Buckley (ed.), *Environmental impacts of ecotourism* (pp. 15–24). Wallingford, Oxon: CABI.

Pomfret, G. (2006). Mountaineering adventure tourists: A conceptual framework for research. *Tourism Management*, 27(1), 113–123.

—. (2011). Package mountaineer tourists holidaying in the French Alps: An evaluation of key influences encouraging their participation. *Tourism Management*, 32(3), 501–510.

—. (2012). Personal emotional journeys associated with adventure activities on packaged mountaineering holidays. *Tourism Management Perspectives*, 4, 145–154.

Robinson, D.W. (1992). A Descriptive model of enduring risk recreation involvement. *Journal of Leisure Research*, 24(1), 52–63.

Rogerson, C.M. (2007). The challenges of developing adventure tourism in South Africa. *Africa Insight,* 37(2), 228–244.

Sung, H.Y., Morrison, A.M., & O'Leary, J. (1996). Definition of adventure travel: Conceptual framework for empirical application from the providers' perspective. In *Proceedings of the Annual Society of Travel and Tourism Educators Conference.* Otawa, Canada.

Swarbrooke, J., Beard, C., Leckie, S., & Pomfret, G. (2003). *Adventure tourism: A new frontier.* Oxford: Elsevier.

Tveit, M., Ode, Å., & Fry, G. (2006). Key concepts in a framework for analysing visual landscape character. *Landscape Research,* 31(3), 229–255.

Urry, J., & Larsen, J. (2011). *The Tourist Gaze 3.0.* London: Sage.

Uysal, M., & Jurowski, C. (1994). Testing the push and pull factors. *Annals of Tourism Research,* 21(4), 844–846.

Varley, P. (2006). Confecting adventure and playing with meaning: The adventure commodification continuum. *Journal of Sport & Tourism,* 11(2), 173–194.

Walle, A.H. (1997). Pursuing risk or insight. *Marketing Adventures,* 24(2), 265–282.

Williams, P., & Soutar, G. (2005). Close to the " edge ": Critical issues for adventure tourism operators. *Asia Pacific Jounral of Tourism Research,* 10(3), 37–41.

Williams, P., & Soutar, G. N. (2009). Value, satisfaction and behavioral intentions in an adventure tourism context. *Annals of Tourism Research,* 36(3), 413–438.

Wu, C. H.-J., & Liang, R.-D. (2011). The relationship between white-water rafting experience formation and customer reaction: a flow theory perspective. *Tourism Management,* 32(2), 317–325.

CHAPTER EIGHT

THE APPEARANCE AND DEVELOPMENT OF SKI RESORTS IN FRANCE

CLAUDE SOBRY AND SORINA CERNAIANU

Abstract

With the largest ski resorts area in Europe and the biggest number of ski lifts facilities in the world, France ranks among the first countries every year in terms of skier visits. The development of skiing in France went through successive steps before the number of skiers stabilized – and the offer diversified vigorously. This chapter describes and analyses the causes of the appearance and development of ski resorts in France from the end of the 19th century to present, trying to submit the phases that this country followed to become the world's top skiing destination. **Keywords**: ski resorts, sports tourism, winter sports, France.

8.1. Introduction

Over winter 2012–2013, France ranked as first country in terms of skiers visits for the second time in a row, with 57.9 million skiers visits (+4.9% in one year), before the United States (56.9 million) and Austria (54.2 million). Out of all figures, 68% of the visitors were French and 32% were foreigners, especially from Europe (Domaines Skiables de France, 2013). France has the biggest number of ski lifts facilities representing 18% of worldwide capacity (Cabinet Architecture et Territoire, 2005). We can notice that on 2nd December 1955, *Le Figaro*, a famous French newspaper, wrote: *"Today France possess the highest cable railway in the world which reaches 3842 meters at his arrival station [...] France possess the longest mileage in ski lifts, distributed in all the mountain resorts and in the most modern, the most powerful, the most capable systems, on 1000 m. of difference in height to take up more than 2500 skiers a day."*.

Today, with 1618 km^2, France has still the largest ski resorts area in Europe which represents 1.4% by the French mountainous surface and counts 3595 lifts among 325 ski areas of which 233 have more than 4 lifts (Vanat, 2013).

How did this country become a world leader in winter sports, when the mountains allowing the practice of skiing only cover a small part of the territory? To answer this question we must go back in time. Indeed, the development of skiing in France went through successive steps before the number of skiers stabilized and the offer diversified vigorously. This chapter describes and analyses the causes of the appearance and development of ski resorts in France from the end of the 19th century to present, trying to submit the phases that this country followed to become the world's top skiing destination.

8.2. The Historical Context

The upper class from the second half of the 19th and beginning of the 20th century took an active part in the development of sports tourism in general, and winter sports in particular. English thermal towns blossomed during the 18th century, offering the gentry all the refined entertainment normally reserved to the upper class: concerts, balls, receptions, games, courtesy *rendezvous*. England had been strongly influenced by Romanticism. Going to the mountains was extraordinarily prestigious, and the hilly landscapes of Bath or the Scottish and Welsh mountains were pale in comparison with the grandiose sites of the Continent – the Alps and Apennine Mountains (Boyer, 2000).

From 1802, English tourists started to massively converge to the other side of the Channel. They were thought to be about a hundred thousand by the end of the 1830's, half a million by 1882 and more than a million by the end of the century. In everyone's mind, France had become a sensational country that had to be visited. However, the tourists first turned to Switzerland. The railway going to Geneva since 1858 played a key role in this fashion for Swiss villages - even though the culture and ideology also played their part in attracting the crowds. For many, Geneva was a mere stop-over on their way to Chamonix.

The pleasure found in physical activity itself comes from Evangelism - the tough version of Christianity – as well as a quest for a top physical condition, which virtually turned into an obsession after Charles Darwin.

During the Georgian era, the aristocrats went on a *Grand Tour,* essentially to discover the pleasures of the flesh (Porter, 1995). The Victorians then went seeking for rest, knowledge, moral progress, health and good physical condition. They found in trekking and climbing their need for hard exercises, healthy activities and moral challenges.

Jacques Balmat and Doctor Michel Paccard reached the top of Mont Blanc for the first time on August 8th, 1786, following the idea of scientist De Saussure who wanted to measure it on July 15th, 1865, and thus originated what would later be called mountain climbing. But it is however George Spencer Matthews, Adolphus Warburton Moore, Horace Walker, Franck Walker, Melchior Anderegg and Jakob Anderegg who first managed to reach the top via the Brenva spur.

English female climber Isabella Straton was the first to climb it in winter conditions, on January 31st, 1876. In 1851, mountain guide Murray claimed that many of those who climbed Mont Blanc had a disturbed mind, and mountain climbing was still considered an eccentric activity. This idea came to a change in 1857 with the creation of the Alpine Club, opening the golden age of mountain climbing.

On 8th August, 1865, Edward Whymper, Lord Francis Douglas, Hadow, Hudson and mountain guide Croz (who died on the way down) climbed on top of the Alps' last virgin peak, mount Cervin. Croz had already climbed Mont Blanc with William Matthews in 1860, and in five years he achieved an impressive amount of prestigious first times – accompanying the best amateurs of his time, mostly English. A stay in the mountains also meant a direct, positive impact on health.

English doctors then advised their rich patients to seek for fresh air in the mountains: "Mountains in summer mean fresh air, spring water, sports, visits and excursions". Seizing the opportunity, ancient mountain villages living from livestock farming turned to new economic activities – balneology (Barège, Cauterets, Luchon, Le Mont-Dore and Saint-Gervais in France), mountain climbing (Chamonix), vacations (Villars). The most prestigious sites of the Alpine mountain range are also the ones with the best facilities, especially on the Mont Blanc (Boyer, 2000).

8.2.1. The development of ski resorts in France

Armed with their new facilities, some resorts intended to attract their summer guests during the winter season, and thus invented the "winter sports" vacations. The English led the way. These resorts offered various sports: ice-skating, sledging, curling, but especially downhill skiing, the only recognized type of skiing at the time ("Downhill only", wrote Arnold Lunn, son of the first travel agent) even though the instructors and equipment were Norwegian. Scandinavian disciplines remained in their original countries, as well as in the massifs of the Vosges and the Jura. The resorts of Megève, Chamonix, Saint-Gervais, and Revard (near Aix-les-Bains) were reserved to wealthy clients.

Whereas summer resorts turned to skiing one after the other (Rauch, 1995), other resorts were directly issued from winter sports activities. The very first being Megève, which was created by the Rotschild family after the first World War in order to cure the soldiers victims of chemical weapons. Megève also saw the very first chair lift, the Mont d'Arbois. Other resorts such as Sestrières, the Alpes d'Huez or Meribel – originated by the English – were created *ex nihilo*.

If the first resorts, situated at a low altitude, had a poor snow-covering who rendered the practice of skiing rather random, the increasing taste for winter sports led mountain villages to invest in hotels, lifts and chalets. We have to bear in mind that at that time, before going for frenzy downhill (on slopes that had not been prepared) the skiers had to climb up the mountain by foot or using sealskin. To make it easier, chair lifts started to appear after 1924. Pomagalski invented the bottom lift in 1935. The idea of creating high altitude resorts – like Sestrières, Italy – came up after 1930. Thus the resorts of Val d'Isère and l'Alpe d'Huezamong others – were built before the Second World War, when the only important post-war construction was Courchevel. That period just saw the modernization of major resorts (Val d'Isère, Alpe d'Huez, Megève, Chamonix, Superbagnères) as well as other smaller and older resorts (les Contamines, Morzine, La Clusaz, Valloire).

We can easily date the development of this snow business (Arnaud & Terret, 1993; Di Ruzza & Gerbier, 1977). The end of the 50s was marked by a series of events showing that the attitude of the marketing sphere, who had not really been involved in the market so far, changed radically. This sudden interest was based on several factors, including:

- in 1957, the tourism committee estimated that the number of visitors for winter sports resorts had increased by 20% per year over the past two years; following these statistics the Conseil Général de Savoie decided to create the resort of Les Ménuires;
- more and more studies focused on the snow business, all showing great optimism as for the vigour of this market, hence the decision in 1959 and 1960 to create the resorts of Flaine and Les Arcs, then La Plagne and Avoriaz (then called Super-Morzine);
- in 1959 a pool of suppliers for the French Ski Team was created and in 1960 Jean Vuarnet won an amazing victory in the Olympic downhill event of Squaw Valley;
- the Government Tourism Advisory Service then decided to list all

ski domains and to allow important grants to equip the mountains in tourist facilities; thus, the public authorities triggered estate investments in the mountains.

From then on, the importance of the role played by the state in the development of the snow business never decreased. Indeed, the State intervened directly by financing the building of resorts such as les Ménuires, Orcières-Merlette, Les Orres, Les Sept-Laux, etc., but also indirectly by allowing private funds to access low-interest mortgages regarding hostel trade and lift construction. Other budgets were also allowed to create access roads.

To understand why the State is that interested in the snow business, we must focus on one particular observation: each resort creation sees the combined intervention of two kinds of economical agents – the Public Work companies and the business banks, the actors changing following the needs. This is what would later be called the "snow cartel", this term also involving the State. The laudatory declarations of public authorities towards the development of this new activity clearly show the hope in a possible and necessary reconversion of the capital, grounded by the post – war reconstruction, as well as the loss of new horizons due to global decolonization.

We also have to notice that the development of mountain facilities did not respect the environment at all.

Up to 1968 existed an official classification for winter sports resorts. Appearing on this list – in other words being of "international standard" – meant having the priority on budget grants and construction permits, and getting the taxes back on ski lifts. It came out that only three resorts could figure on this list, as the others did not meet the requirements regarding water treatment – one of the requirements for this classification. So be it, the law was modified in the end of November, 1968, allowing these resorts to be on the list provided that they would set up a water cleaning system within five years.

We must also focus on the Olympics held in Grenoble in 1968. At first reluctant, the public authorities–led by the government–backed up the city's application and granted it an important budget for developing and transforming the economy of Isère, this region then shifting from a critical economy based on small agricultural exploitations, to a tourism–based economy. These Games were clearly expected to have a positive impact on developing winter tourism – this term being limited to the mere notion of winter sports, and winter sports itself being centred on downhill ski only, the only profitable discipline. As for media coverage, these Winter Games were the first to be broadcasted in colour – the Grenoble Games following the policy developed in the last ten years aiming at developing winter sports (Frappat, 1991).

The objective of development of the ski domain planned during the 1960s-70s was to set up "money traps". The construction of third generation resorts (then still called "resort towns") had for actual goal to boost real estate, a vector for the financial sphere. The first consequence of the development of these resorts was the hyper-development of secondary residences, at the expense of hostelry.

Following H. Bonnet (former coach for the men's downhill ski team), and J-C. Killy (1976) (three times gold medal in the Games of Grenoble, 1968), "Some governmental and tourist authorities, shaken by the moment's euphoria, decided that mountain hostelry had to be industrial. As a consequence, for some time, the budget was only granted to future hotels that would bear more than 40 rooms. And thus led to the end of family hostelry [...]. Moreover, attracted by the Dollar and strong currencies, tourism services were only hoping for three-star hotels so as to attract the foreigners – and especially the Americans – hence the lack of diversity in the modern resorts' hostelry [...]. Buildings, flats and studios of all sizes and shapes then replaced the hotels that no one could build anymore [...]. The estate agencies naturally took over hostelry [...]". "Mountains have become a financial value. That's why local populations are evicted and taken away from their roots, to ensure the construction of mass-tourism areas within unspoilt sites, in favour of the upper class.", said Rabinovitch (1973). Important investments – encouraged and backed up by the government bearing all expenses regarding road accesses, and above all sanitation – were built up on perspectives of high rentability, essentially – or entirely–based on international and/or wealthy tourists, as well as the perspective of a mountain economy strengthened by these new activities, the creation of thousands of jobs and new incomes. In reality, the consequences were the destructuring of mountain economy, and the locals' situation changing from independent mountain farmers to salaried workers.

The profits issued from winter sports development barely went to the locals, at least proportionally.

This upper–class designed policy, with consequences on territory planning – the resorts aiming at attracting more the "long–stay" skiers rather than the "week end" skiers via precise geographical characteristics-was soon to meet its limits especially because this type of clients, always looking for innovation, turns to sea and sun during the off–season.

The first symptoms of the market's bursting point were perceived during winter 1970–71. The States' policy was then rapidly modified, public investments more in favour of the diversification of real estate, a direction then followed by the promoters. The goal was to attract more clients by becoming available to the middle-class. In concrete terms, this "democratization" led to the improvement of various resorts – generally by enlarging an existing village instead of building new resorts *ex nihilo*, closer to the urban areas and for cheaper costs. It had a double effect: first, the resorts were at a lower altitude compared to the preceding era and secondly cross–country skiing was developed, as it was technically more affordable – and thus available to a potentially wider range of customers. But the retreat of public authorities and promoters, little or not interested at all, put the resorts in a precarious financial situation despite the ski domains requiring less facilities.

This new approach had heavy consequences on the two following decades. Poor practice conditions, longer queues at the lift stations, the villages multiplying the number of beds without increasing the customers' transport capacity, the opening of aerial space allowing to travel cheap and escape the crowds invading the slopes and the resorts concentrating on skiing only, a fact highlighted by the low amount of snow coverage at the end of the 80s (1988, 89, 90). Satellite resorts as well interconnected ski areas increasingly complex begin to appear. A number of small resorts, so–called "family resorts", were endangered because of the insufficient snow, the high costs of snowmaking as well the rivalry neighbouring resorts.

8.3. Methodology

As mentioned previously, this chapter tries to present an historical and economic approach of the development of ski resorts in France, highlighting the multiple stages in the development of this, always considered as a higher class activity when, in the same time, the development of ski resorts has been and still is used to develop some regions by receiving more tourists.

Our research is based especially on a bibliographic documentation coming from the last 30 years (books, articles, Internet sources) and statistical data providing by DSF (Domaines skiables de France) which is an organization representing the French ski industry and operate since 1938. The real purpose of the chapter is to understand why and how French ski resorts are today the first in the world for the number of received tourists when France is not considered as a mountain country like Austria.

8.4. Results

Gradual modernization and diversification of tourism infrastructure and ski facilities in winter resorts positively influenced the evolution of tourism activity in France which was reflected in the substantial increase of the number of tourists.

The last year's data analysis shows an increase of skier visits after the 2006/2007 season (see Figure 8.1) was affected by a serious lack of snow. The negative impact of the lack of snowfall on tourist arrival in mountain resorts was reduced and the ski areas were well adapted to these scenario. 21% of French ski slopes area (which has 26581 ha) has snowmaking equipment (Domaines skiables de France, 2013).

One of the decisive factors to practice skiing is the existence of good ski slopes. For this point of view France is particularly advantaged concerning its variety and quality.

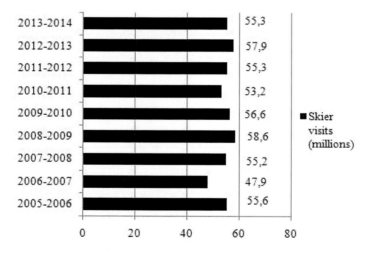

Figure 8.1 – Evolution of skier-visits

Because of climate change France develops and implements responsible policies concerning the improvement of human, environmental and technical conditions. Every year 300 million euro is invested to maintain and renew the ski facilities (Domaines skiables de France, 2012).

A report realized by L. Vanat (2014) on snow and mountain tourism shows that of the three countries with more than 50 million skier-visits (calculated as the average of the 5 last seasons, or estimate) Austria registered the biggest national participation rate (in % population) (36%), followed by France (13%) and USA (4.3%). Moreover, the ratio of foreign skiers in Austria is 66%, 32% in France and 5.6% in USA (see Table 8.1).

Table 8.1 – Figures about skiing for the countries

Country	Skier visits[1]	National participation rate (in % population)	Number of skiers (national)	Proportion of foreign skiers (%)
USA	57,092,127	4.3	13,616,748	5.6
France	56,226,000	13	8,573,709	32
Austria	53,155,600	36	2,959,793	66

[1] Average of the 5 last seasons, or estimate.
Source: Vanat, 2014.

The heads for winter sports resorts and tourism, now aware of the rise of an international rivalry – be it in winter sports or in tourism in general –, started to reconsider their offer. Thirty years of efforts and investments were necessary for France to be back among the skiers' world favourite destinations, and take the lead as welcoming country in this field.

The tourists are back due to various factors, among which figures the unique *savoir-faire* of the *Compagnie des Alpes* – world leader in ski domain exploitation – which now brings resorts in every country bearing mountains and a developing middle-class.

8.4.1. The development of new winter sports

The rebound of winter sports in France went through the enlargement of the customer base – as 75% of the customers are French and mainly coming from the middle–class – and the diversification of the offer.

If for a long time the efforts were targeting the lifts and infrastructures, now the main focus is on the superstructure, image, reputation and attractiveness of a site. *"Popular winter sports turn the mountains into a gigantic leisure centre", "The Alps have become an amusement park"*, there are so many opinions – sometimes rather bitter – about the evolution of the offer. Although yesterday the main concern was to offer means to go *up* the mountains, today it is all about developing ways to go *down* the slopes. Even if the skiing remains the main tourist activity, the offer for leisure activities is getting more diverse: snow shoes, fat bikes, yooners, paragliding, and mushing. The goal is also to impress –next to the lifts appear more and more giant spas, issued from considerable investments: 11.6 million euro for Aquariaz (Avoriaz), 62 million euro for the water park in Courchevel. It is the price to pay for the tourists to go "Wow!". All resorts want to be different from their rivals by offering exclusive forms of entertainment. They have to work on their international image as a brand, just as any other product. In that way they highlight the qualities of the site and sterilize a hostile environment to fulfil the customers' expectations. For instance, Courchevel resort spends $40,000 a day for snow removal – 45 million dollars a year – but sells for 75 million dollars in passes every year. Digital technologies also have an essential role: 70% of the customers plan their winter holidays online, and 56% of them book them on the internet. The resorts also hire "net watchers" who follow the social media in order to solve the (big or small) problems met by the tourists. Web sharing platforms have been set up and social networks like Facebook are used by the professionals to follow the opinion of their "friends". The users also have the possibility to find their friends and chat with them via an iPhone application. A mask allows them to read all information about the domain in real-time – the weather, open or closed slopes, quality of the snow or even their own performances.

When some welcome those investments, others blame the standardization and artificialization of the landscapes, and the threatening of the cultural identity and traditional economic activities. The investments concerning the Alps on the European level are also feared to be blind, desperate and helpless for two reasons:

- the market of snow has come to an end; the number of Western, middle-class skiers does not increase anymore, and the amount of children learning how to ski decreases because of high prices;
- the observed and forecasted global warming induces very expensive investments, which lead to increasing the prices of "snow" products – and thus diminishing the targeted customer base.

Then we assist to a high money-making situation which profitability is now stagnant and will tend to decrease, and with an increasing rivalry between the resorts who try to drag as many customers as they can – which can only be done at the expense of other resorts. Some of them are bound to disappear; the investments are still money-making, but their profitability is decreasing.

For winter sports investors, the future lays somewhere else, as the market is getting global and develops in every country seeing the appearance of a middle class. Thus, this future resides in Georgia, Azerbaijan, Caucasus – where Northern Caucasus Resorts is currently building five resorts (the first one, Sochi, held the 2014 Winter Olympics, with a construction cost of 50 million Euros) using the technology sold by N. Sarkozy to V. Putin in 2010 – as well as in China (with 2 million skiers today and an estimated 20 million in 2020) where the slopes are 100% covered with artificial snow, causing environmental damage and why not even in Lesotho, Southern Africa, where the Austrians have built the resort *Afriski* with 150 beds and plans for more, aiming at attracting the South African upper class.

8.5. Conclusion

Thirty years of efforts and investments were necessary for France to be back among the skiers' top world destinations - and even reach the first place for welcoming countries. The awareness of the evolution of international rivalry whether in the field of winter sports itself or in tourism in general led the tourism and resorts managers to reconsider their offer of "snow products" (Clary, 1993).Today it's the whole French industry of winter sports, mostly through *Domaines skiables de France*, which exports all over the world the "know-how" obtained by more than fifty years of experience in a very evolutionary market. The change of climate and the development of new markets redistribute cards. The traditional European resorts see the profitability of always higher investment decreasing. Some of them will probably disappear in the next years (as already did some resorts of low or average height because of the lack of snow). They must diversify their offer to attract the customers, mostly the foreign customers always looking for novelties and the best value for money on a worldwide market.

References

ATOUT France (2009). *Les chiffres clés du tourisme en montagne* (7th ed.). Paris: ATOUT France.

Arnaud, P., & Terret, T. (1993). *Le rêve blanc; olympisme et sport d'hiver en France, Chamonix 1924 – Grenoble 1968*. Bordeaux: Presses Universitaires de Bordeaux.

Boyer, M. (2000). *Histoire de l'invention du tourisme, XVIé – XIXé siècles*. La tour d'Aigues: Éditions de L'Aube.

Cabinet Architecture et Territoire (2005). *Le positionnement de l'offre Française de sports d'hiver. Note de Synthèse*. Retrieved from http://www.tourisme.gouv.fr/stat_etudes/etudes/territoires/offre_sports _hiver.pdf

Clary, D. (1993). *Le tourisme dans l'espace français*. Paris: Masson.

Di Ruzza, F., & Gerbier, B. (1977). *Ski en crise. Essai sur l'économie du sport*. Grenoble: Presses Universitaires de Grenoble, p. 41.

Domaines skiables de France (2013). *Indicateurs et analyses 2013*. L'Observatoire. Retrieved from http://www.domaines-skiables.fr/ index.php?option=com_content&task=view&id=223&Itemid=157

Frappat, P. (1991). Les Jeux Olympiques à Grenoble: une ville industrielle saisie par le sport. in *Revue internationale de l'arc alpin*, Jeux Olympiques d'hiver: montagne et développement, 3, Tome LXXIX.

Killy, J-C., & Bonnet, H. (1976). *Le ski*. Paris: Denoël, p. 23.

Porter, R. (1995). *Les anglais et les loisirs*. in Alin Corbin, *L'avènement des loisirs, 1850 – 1960*, Paris: Aubier, p. 21.

Rabinovitch, W. (1973). Le marché de la neige, in *Revue Esprit,*1, Paris.

Rauch, A. (1995). *Les vacances et la nature revisitée*. in Alin Corbin, *L'avènement des loisirs, 1850 – 1960*, Paris: Aubier, p. 83.

Vanat, L. (2014). *2014 International Report on Snow & Mountain Tourism. Overview of the key industry figures for ski resorts*. Retrieved from http://www.vanat.ch/6665.html

Chapter Nine

Appreciative Inquiry: A Promising Research Tool for Rural Tourism Management

Roslizawati Che Aziz, Mohani Abdul, Yuhanis Abdul Aziz and Azmawani Abd Rahman

Abstract

Rural tourism is now an important developmental agenda and is a strong and growing sector in the global tourism market. The protection of nature coupled with economic growth, improvements in the built–environment, and development of infrastructure are the most significant contributions of this sector. Rural tourism has become a major force in rural economic development and therefore deserves further investment. Moreover, it not only contributes towards alleviating poverty in rural communities but has generated large–scale employment opportunities for the rural inhabitants. With this in mind, the Appreciative Inquiry (AI) is a recent approach used in tourism research and has been identified as a new research tool for evaluating the contributions of rural tourism. **Keywords:** appreciative inquiry, rural tourism, tourism development.

9.1. Introduction

Within the travel industry, rural tourism has become an important developmental agenda for many countries due to its potential to provide tangible benefits to communities that have few means of contributing to the global economy. Rural tourism is considered a strong and growing sector in the global tourism market. The protection and improvement of natural and built environments along with developments in infrastructure led to socio–cultural development are therefore are the most significant contributions of this sector (Lo, Mohamad, Songan, & Yeo, 2012).

In remote areas, tourism is ideally developed using the inherent characteristics and resources of the locality that are based on "their attractive natural environment, original local culture and traditional systems of land use and farming" (Bramwell & Lane, 2012). The purpose and significance of developing rural tourism is rooted in its major influence on rural economic development. It contributes toward poverty alleviation among the rural communities. Large-scale employment opportunities for the rural dwellers are known to result from rural tourism. More importantly, rural tourism has been transforming rural economies but needs to be supported and promoted by relevant policies to ensure continued success (World Tourism Organisation, 2001).

Developing rural tourism does not mean letting go of local culture and traditions, in fact it may assist in preserving the local cultural, social and environment (Lo *et al.*, 2012). The potential of developing tourism activities in rural areas cannot be over-emphasized. More than just economic benefits are received by local communities from tourism activities; biodiversity conservation results from the synergy between tourism development (Marsden & Smith, 2005). Due to this synergy, an integrated framework or model for maximizing benefits from tourism development is needed to show how tourism can directly support community development and conservation efforts (García-Rosell & Mäkinen, 2012).

Awareness about the environment and providing intensive training for income-generating activities, particularly in remote areas, would involve capacity building of the communities. Thus, the development of tourism in rural communities requires high value placed on sustainability and awareness of economic development, sustainability and the fragile environment (Diao, 2012; Johnson, 2010). Thus, it is important to resolve these issues that are being raised by analysing the literature related to rural tourism development and the significance of sustainable development in the tourism industry.

However, being constrained by remoteness and underdevelopment, rural areas still have limited options for economic development. This study seriously disagrees with the assertion put forward by Liu (2006) that to stimulate economic progress in rural areas, they must inevitably seek alternative uses of their local resources. This is not necessarily the case because, in fact, there have been few discussions about the contribution of tourism at the rural community level. According to Koster and Lemelin (2009), two gaps have been identified in rural tourism and its contribution to development; how to make rural tourism a viable industry in resource-dependent communities and how to embed the industry within a community seeking alternatives from crisis context. Given that, the Appreciative Inquiry (AI) approach has therefore been identified as a new research tool for evaluating the impact of rural tourism on community development.

9.2. Literature Review

What does rural tourism mean? For many in the industry, the word rural is a common 'house-ware,' particularly for those who are involved in the development of society. However, in the tourism industry, rural tourism varies considerably from one country to another country. The term occurs in advanced industrial societies. It was born in the mid-1950s when the European economic reconstruction process was completed after the Second World War (Ciolac, Csosz, Merce, Balan, & Dincu, 2011). The term rural tourism has been a subject of discussion either in a policy context or in literature. But such definitions do little to convey the true meaning of tourism in rural areas because of the difficulty of establishing what is 'rural'.

In a broader direction, Bramwell and Lane (2012) and Lane (1994) have discussed and established the purest form of rural tourism, which includes few elements (see Figure 9.1).

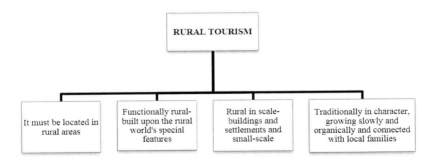

Figure 9.1 – Definition of rural tourism
Source: Bramwell & Lane, 2012; Lane, 1994.

In much of the recent literature on the tourism industry, efforts have been made to define the term of rural tourism itself. The literature related to rural tourism areas are heterogeneous and the definition of a rural area is thus problematic (Holland, Burian, Dixey, & Goodwin, 2003; Pakurar & Olah, 2008). The different terminologies are used according to their aims or types of activities in rural areas such as adventure, eco-tourism and green tourism (Polo & Frías, 2010).

In particular, Knowd (2001) asserts that experience plays an important role in defining the term of rural tourism. The rural character of places such as its attraction and characteristics may assist in a better understanding of rural tourism. It is believed that the definition is still heterogeneous, as rural tourism is generally regarded as including a wide range of elements, products and services provided as well as the location. For instance, the elements of accommodation, activities related to the nature, and traditional and cultural conservation are amongst the tourism products, which have been developed in an area characterized as being rural (Bramwell & Lane, 2012; Lane, 1994).

9.3. Background of the Appreciative Inquiry Approach

The Appreciative Inquiry (AI) approach was first developed in 1986 by David Cooperrider in his doctoral thesis on *"Appreciative Inquiry: Towards a methodology for understanding and enhancing organizational innovation"* (Cooperrider, Whitney, & Stavros, 2008; Cooperrider & Whitney, 2005). It has been practiced around the world for more than a decade by non-profit organizations, businesses, families, health care organizations, schools, as well as governments. Since the late 1980s, AI has been promoted to a wide variety of organizations for many different purposes and applied to strategic planning, culture transformation, increasing customer satisfaction, organization redesign, as well as for leadership development. Even after the successful implementation of the AI approach in the development field, however, it has been irregularly used for research purposes, especially in the field of tourism (Nyaupane & Poudel, 2012; Raymond & Hall, 2008b).

Basically, AI has been developed to gain and build enduring relationships between communities and the tourism industry based on the simple assumption that every organization or community has something that works well and those strengths can be the starting point in creating positive changes (Raymond & Hall, 2008a, 2008b). Previous studies have also defined AI as an alternative approach to problem solving, positioned within a social constructionist framework that builds on positive affirmation of organizational strengths to address workplace issues (Koster & Lemelin, 2009).

When individuals change their inner and explicit dialogues to focus primarily on affirmation and support, they change their stories and their organizations for the better (Cooperrider & Whitney, 2005; Judy & Hammond, 2006). Additionally, AI can be used to develop plans and commitment in which organizational members collectively define the best of 'what is' and has been used to create provocative possibilities and plans for the future. The process builds positive affirmation and alignment for commitment (Cooperrider *et al.*, 2008).

By seeking out the best of *'what is'* to help ignite the collective imagination of *'what might be'*, AI aims to generate new knowledge that expands the *'realm of possibility'*. It also helps individuals, groups and organizations envision a collective desired future and to carry forth that vision in ways that successfully translate images of possibility into reality and belief into practice (Cooperrider & Whitney, 2005). Indeed, the AI process engages the entire community and its stakeholders to create a future that works for everyone. It can be used to guide conservation, large group meetings or a whole–system effort (Finegold, Holland, & Lingham, 2002; Shariff, Gramberg, & Foley, 2009).

No matter what the purpose is, the Appreciative Inquiry 4-D Cycle is the foundation for change. The essence of all these models is based on a set of principles which generally follow the framework of the 4-D Cycle (Figure 9.2). Each AI process is home-grown and designated to meet the unique challenges of the organization and the industry involved (Cooperrider & Whitney, 2005).

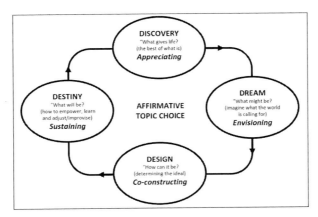

Figure 9.2 – The Appreciative Inquiry 4-D Cycle
Source: Cooperrider & Whitney, 2005, p.16.

The four key phrases of an AI process, illustrated in Figure 9.2, are as follows:

Discovery: At the heart of discovery is the appreciative interview where the uniqueness and power of AI stems from its fundamentally affirmative focus. At this phase, what distinguishes AI is that every question is positive. People also uncover at this stage what gives life to their organization, department, or community when it is at its best (ibid. p.25).

Dream: This stage calls for people to listen carefully to the moments of the organization when it was at its best and to share images of their hopes and dreams for their collective future. At this stage, its main purpose is to engage the whole system in moving beyond the status quo to envision a valued and vital future (ibid. p.27).

Design: During this stage, people are invited to challenge the status quo, as well as the common assumptions underlying the design of their organization. They are encouraged to wonder beyond the data with the essential question: "What would our organization look like if it were designed in every way possible to maximize the qualities of the positive core?" (ibid. p.28).

Destiny: This phrase specifically applies to personal and organizational commitments and the paths forward (Whitney & Trosten-Bloom, 2010), delivers on the new images of the future and is sustained by nurturing a collective sense of purpose. Building an *"appreciative eye"* into all of the organization's systems, procedures and ways of working is key to sustaining momentum (Cooperrider *et al.*, 2008). The phase of destiny is ongoing and brings the organization back to the discovery phase, in which continues its application of the method that may result in new topic choices, dialogues, and continued learning.

9.3.1. The distinctiveness of the appreciative inquiry approach

AI development has recently found that the process does not only help an organization to create images of the future, but also to create and nurture energy, a renewed commitment to change, and a sense of hope among people working to achieve the future (Calabrese, Hester, Friesen, & Burkhalter, 2010; Michael, 2005). The AI approach has emerged in order to counter traditional problem-solving approaches because it focuses on the strengths and successes of individuals, organizations and communities

(Cooperrider *et al.*, 2008). In a shift from the traditional approach of identifying, analysing and solving problems, AI builds on the strengths of organizations or communities to develop a positive approach in addressing issues (Raymond & Hall, 2008b).

What makes AI different from other approaches can be discussed in various ways. Many other existing participatory change strategies have been used in various settings with varying degrees of success. Predominantly, AI is focusing on local strengths and achievements, encouraging local participation and emphasizing local knowledge rather than deficits and problems. While other kind of approaches such as the top–down approach and even the participatory–led approach, these often proceeded by defining needs, problems, and obstacles in an organization or community and lacked appreciation of their strengths and successes (Laszlo & Cooperrider, 2010). In Table 9.1, the significant strength of the AI approach in comparison to other traditional approaches is highlighted.

Table 9.1 – The Power of AI Approach

Problem solving approach	Appreciative Inquiry approach
"Felt Need" Identification of Problem	Appreciating "Valuing the Best of What Is"
Analysis of Causes	Envisioning "What Might Be"
Analysis of Possible Solutions	Dialoguing "What Should Be"
Action Planning (Treatment)	Innovating "What will Be"
Organization is a problem to be solved	Organization is a mystery (infinite capacity) to be embraced

Source: Cooperrider & Whitney, 2005, p.13.

The initiators of AI have regarded these approaches as "*problem-solving*" or "*deficit-based*" in development, and considered them an alternative. The problem–solving as well as the deficit–based approaches tend to leave people with the impression that their community is full of problems and needs, many of which require the help of outside experts to overcome (Cooperrider & Whitney, 2005). The main theme of the deficit–based approach is to solve problems and the questions normally will begin like "*What is wrong?*" and "*What is the problem?*"

As a method of organizational analysis, AI differs from conventional managerial problem solving. The basic underlying assumption of AI is that an organization is a "*solution to be embraced*" rather than a "*problem to be solved*" (Cooperrider et al., 2008). In contrast, the basic assumption of problem solving is that "*organizing is a problem to be solved*". Often, these approaches also failed to sustain participation and commitment of local people. Hence, it always places emphasis on fixing problems in a community (Judy & Hammond, 2006). Cooperrider *et al.* (2008) assert that the task of improvement traditionally involves removing deficits by identifying the key problems or deficiencies, analysing the causes, analysing solutions, and developing an action plan.

Appreciative Inquiry has been embraced as a powerful organization development philosophy building on past success to propel positive changes. AI is a highly participatory and holistic approach to change the values held by members of the organization and amplifies positive forces within it (Bellinger & Elliott, 2011). Researchers and practitioners of AI have developed eight foundational principles to help understand its implementation and functions (Preskill & Catsambas, 2006). They claim that these eight principles arise from several disparate theories.

Related research studies focus on the effects of positive thinking and images. These unique principles are as special as their derivative practices (Whitney & Trosten-Bloom, 2010) and move the basis of AI from theory to practice (Cooperrider et al., 2008; Cooperrider & Whitney, 2005; Whitney & Trosten-Bloom, 2010):

- The Constructionist Principle (*the way we know is fateful*),
- The Principle of Simultaneity (*change begins at the moment you ask the question*),
- The Poetic Principle (*we can choose what we study*),
- The Anticipatory Principle (*change in active images of the future*),
- The Positive Principle (*positive questions lead to positive change*),
- The Wholeness Principle (*wholeness brings out the best*),
- The Enactment Principle (*acting 'as if' is self-fulfilling*),
- The Free Choice Principle (*free choice liberates power*).

In keeping with the spirit of AI, an inquiry into *why Appreciative Inquiry works* was provided by Whitney and Trosten-Bloom (2010). They created a set of questions, helped focus groups, and conducted formal and informal interviews in several organizations—most notably Hunter Douglas Window Fashion Division. The key findings of their study found that AI works by generating six essential conditions within an organization. These conditions through which AI liberates power and unleashes human potential are called the Six Freedoms. The following is the list of Six Freedoms by Whitney and Trosten-Bloom (2010):

-   AI creates a context in which people are "free to be known in relationship".
-   AI makes a space in which people are "free to be heard".
-   AI opens the opportunity for people to be "free to dream in community".
-   AI establishes an environment where people are "free to choose to contribute".
-   AI provides the context for people to be "free to act with support".
-   AI opens the way for people to be "free to be positive".

With that, it is believed that AI works as it unleashes all of the Six Freedoms over the course of the 4–D Cycle. It creates a surge of power, energy, and self–perpetuating momentum for a positive change. As discussed earlier, AI has been used as a theoretical research approach and the research methodology is through positive inquiry in order to initiate community/organizational change. It takes the best from the past and present to create the future in order to provide the basis for constructing an image of what could be and should become the collectively co–constructed design for the organization (Cooperrider & Whitney, 2005).

As the people within an organization learn to value each other, synergy is created that will drive the organization forward in a positive way. Hence, the energy of people within an organization is led towards discovering the positive core and the power it holds is used to positively shape the organization or community (Laszlo & Cooperrider, 2010).

9.4. Conclusion

Rural tourism was acknowledged as an economically significant sector of a country's economy and holds great potential in terms of sustainable rural development. It is able to allow rural people to gain the benefits of tourism development while promoting more balanced as well as sustainable forms of development. In fact, it may offer differentiated products to tourists, blending them together with nature and appreciation of culture at a particular destination. This is the main focus of rural tourism as rural areas are rich in natural and cultural traditional elements.

Besides that, rural tourism also promotes the preservation of various products that are nature-based, community centred, and rooted in the local environment. However, such definitions of rural tourism do little to convey the true concepts of rural tourism because the difficulty of establishing what is 'rural'. The key features that make rural tourism relevant to rural development are poverty and lack of economic opportunities, combined with the natural resources, scenic and cultural aspect of the area, which provides tourism assets. Therefore, the true concepts may vary based on study frames. Any concept of rural tourism that needs to recognize the essential and contextual qualities of what is 'rural'.

It is believed that all over the world the notion of rural tourism has meant different things for different people. As it is a normative term therefore, different forms of concepts and definitions of rural tourism have assumed a complexity of the activity. In rural areas, tourism plays an important role in local lives that can positively influence regional development or vice- versa. Everywhere across the world, the aim of rural tourism is not just to increase the net benefits to rural people from the tourism industry but also to enhance the participation of local people in managing tourism products. Therefore, if more tourism can be developed and well preserved, the poverty impacts amongst local people in rural areas can be reduced.

However, since 1986, the AI approach has been applied in the field of community development especially in developing countries. Therefore, with this in mind, it has been identified as an alternative tourism research tool for evaluating the impacts of rural tourism for sustainable development. AI is one of the recent approaches used in tourism research, particularly at the community level. The AI 4–D Cycle serves as the foundation on which change is built, including Discover (appreciating and valuing), Dream (envisioning), Design (co–constructing the future) and Destiny (learning, empowering and improvising to sustain the future).

The approach is typically used to facilitate positive developments and may be used within the tourism industry. As a research method, AI acts as an alternative to the conventional action research in the organizational development field and it is applicable to the study of tourism. This method seeks the strengths of individuals, organizations, communities, and societies, giving life, health, and excellence to the development of those human systems. Recent AI development has found that the process does not only help an organization to create images of the future, but also to create and nurture energy, a renewed commitment to change, and a sense of hope among its people working to achieve the future.

The AI approach has emerged in order to counter traditional problem-solving approaches. This is because it focuses on the strengths and successes of individuals, organizations, and communities. In a shift from the traditional approach of identifying, analysing, and solving problems, AI builds on the strengths of organizations or communities to develop a positive approach in addressing issues. This method seeks the strengths of individuals, organizations, communities, and societies, giving life, health, and excellence to the development of those human systems. It is believed that there is a significant potential for the adoption of the AI approach within the tourism discipline as it is rarely used in this field. When compared to other approaches, AI addresses organizational issues in a significantly different way. Instead of focusing on the problems and what is not working and why, AI asks its organization members to discover what is working well and what would comply as "the best" within the organization.

References

Bellinger, A., & Elliott, T. (2011). What are you looking at? the potential of appreciative inquiry as a research approach for social work. *British Journal of Social Work, 41*(4), 708–725.

Bramwell, B., & Lane, B. (2012). Towards innovation in sustainable tourism research? *Journal of Sustainable Tourism, 20*(1), 1–7.

Calabrese, R., Hester, M., Friesen, S., & Burkhalter, K. (2010). Using appreciative inquiry to create a sustainable rural school district and community. *International Journal of Educational Management, 24*(3), 250–265.

Ciolac, R., Csosz, I., Merce, I.I., Balan, I., & Dincu, A.M. (2011). Study on the concept of rural tourism and leverage of some specific activities from rural areas through rural tourism. *Scientific Papers: Animal Science and Biotechnologies, 44*(2), 471–474.

Cooperrider, D.L., & Whitney, D. (2005). *Appreciative inquiry: A positive revolution in change.* San Francisco: Berrett-Koehler Publishers.

Cooperrider, D.L., Whitney, D., & Stavros, J.M. (2008). *Appreciative Inquiry Handbook - For Leaders of Change.* In R. Fry (ed.). (2nd ed.). Brunswick, Ohio: Crown Custom Publishing & Berrett-Koehler Publishers.

Diao, Z. (2012). Study on development Patterns of rural tourism in china - problems of rural tourism in China. In *Technology for Education and Learning* (pp.689–693). Berlin: Springer-Verlag Berlin Heidelberg.

Finegold, M.A., Holland, B.M., & Lingham, T. (2002). Appreciative Inquiry and public dialogue: An approach to community change. *Public Organization Review, 2,* 235–252.

García-Rosell, J.-C., & Mäkinen, J. (2012). An integrative framework for sustainability evaluation in tourism: applying the framework to tourism product development in Finnish Lapland. *Journal of Sustainable Tourism,* December, 1–21.

Holland, J., Burian, M., Dixey, L., & Goodwin, H. (2003). *Tourism in poor rural areas: diversifying the product and expanding the benefits in rural Uganda and the Czech Republic* (No. 12). *Social Research* (pp.1–39). Czeh Republic.

Johnson, P.A. (2010). Realizing rural community-based tourism development : Prospects for social-economy enterprises. *Journal of Rural and Community Development, 5*(1), 150–162.

Judy, S., & Hammond, S. (2006). *An introduction to Appreciative Inquiry* (pp.1–12). Argenta, B.C.

Knowd, I. (2001). *Rural tourism: Panacea and paradox* (pp.1–46). Sydney, Australia.

Koster, R.L.P., & Lemelin, R.H. (2009). Appreciative Inquiry and rural tourism: A case study from Canada. *Tourism Geographies, 11*(2), 256–269.

Lane, B. (1994). What is rural tourism? *Journal of Sustainable Tourism, 2*(1-2), 7–21.

Laszlo, C., & Cooperrider, D.L. (2010). Creating sustainable value: A strength-based whole system approach. In T. Thatchenkery, D.L. Cooperrider, & M. Avital (eds.). *Advance in appreciative inquiry-positive design and appreciative construction: From sustainable development to sustainable value* (pp.17–33). Bingley: Emerald.

Liu, A. (2006). Tourism in rural areas: Kedah, Malaysia. *Tourism Management, 27,* 878–889.

Lo, M.-C., Mohamad, A.A., Songan, P., & Yeo, A.W. (2012). Positioning rural tourism: Perspectives from the local communities. *International Journal of Trade, Economic and Finance, 3*(1), 59–65.

Marsden, T., & Smith, E. (2005). Ecological entrepreneurship: Sustainable development in local communities through quality food production and local branding. *Geoforum, 36*(4), 440–451.

Michael, S. (2005). The promise of Appreciative Inquiry as an interview tool for field research. *Development in Practice, 15*(2), 222–230.

Nyaupane, G.P., & Poudel, S. (2012). Application of appreciative inquiry in tourism research in rural communities. *Tourism Management, 33*(4), 978–987.

Pakurar, M., & Olah, J. (2008). Definition of rural tourism and its characteristics in the northern great plain region. *Fascicula: Ecotoxicologie, Zootehni Si Technologii De Industrie Alimentara, 7*(7), 777–782.

Polo, A.I., & Frías, D. (2010). Collective strategies for rural tourism: The experience of networks in Spain. *Journal of Tourism Consumption and Practice, 2*(1), 25–45.

Preskill, H., & Catsambas, T.T. (2006). *Reframing evaluation through Appreciative Inquiry*. Ohio: Sage.

Raymond, E.M., & Hall, C.M. (2008a). The development of cross-cultural (mis)understanding through volunteer. *Journal of Sustainable Tourism, 16*(5), 530–543.

Raymond, E.M., & Hall, C.M. (2008b). The potential for Appreciative Inquiry in tourism research. *Current Issues in Tourism, 11*(3), 281–292.

Shariff, Z., Gramberg, B. Van, & Foley, P. (2009). The usefulness of Appreciative Inquiry as a method to identify mass sports program success. *Transylvanian Review of Administrative Sciences*, (30), 118–131.

Whitney, D., & Trosten-Bloom, A. (2010). *The power of Appreciative Inquiry: A practical guide to positive change*. In D. Cooperrider (ed.). 2nd ed. San Francisco: Berrett-Koehler Publisher.

World Tourism Organisation (2001). *Rural tourism master plan for Malaysia* (pp.1–180). Malaysia.

Chapter Ten

The Sustainability of Health Organizations for Medical Tourism Development

Kivanc Inelmen, Begum Aydin and Mehmet Ulus

Abstract

Medical tourism is a growing segment of the industry that is becoming a choice for patients globally. As an emerging market economy, Turkey has experienced a boom in the last few years in terms of investments in medical care and has developed its potential to become one of the leading medical tourism destinations. At this point, the use of medical tourism as a tool for sustainable development should be explored. Therefore, this chapter aims to determine how health organizations in Istanbul with a medical tourism focus treat sustainability. For the study, a semi-structured survey was deployed, adapting Global Sustainable Tourism Council performance indicators. The impact of medical tourism and its management strategies are revealed, and suggestions for more sustainable management are provided. **Keywords:** sustainability, medical tourism, health organizations, Turkey.

10.1. Introduction

Sustainability has become a buzzword, and while it is widely used in the tourism industry, the meaning varies according to the user: it most often refers to sustainability of profit, occasionally includes an element of environmental friendliness and less frequently refers to socio-cultural sustainability, although technically the term includes all of these aspects. Travelling for medical reasons, however, has existed for thousands of years, sometimes as a sole aim, and sometimes along with activities such as SPA (*salus per aquam*) and wellness or with entertaining activities in warmer, clearer weather. In addition to such indirect expectations of improved healthcare, there is a distinct type of tourism, often referred to as medical tourism, which includes interventions such as surgical procedures in health organizations.

In the past, the direction of medical tourism was from developing countries to the developed to access treatments that were not available in the home country. Recently, however, the tide has reversed. As a high value tourism product, medical tourism now receives the support of governments and is seen globally as a profitable business opportunity by entrepreneurs. Medical tourism combining medical interventions with travel is a growing sector in numerous developing countries, most commonly in the Far East and South America (Mechinda *et al.*, 2010). Although there is a growing trend in mobility worldwide, the effects of medical tourism have not yet been subjected to extensive research. Based on the findings of prior research, it could be argued that medical tourism in countries which have recently become involved in this business is focused primarily on strategies to increase the number of visitor patients and their total expenditures (Erdogan & Yilmaz, 2012).

Today many patients prefer to have medical treatment abroad for reasons ranging from lower costs to lenient laws on organ transplantation and artificial insemination, depending on the country. However, the lack of standardization in medical care, bureaucratic problems related to patients' insurance, payment and follow-up, as well as difficulties in reporting and initiating legal procedures in the event of malpractice are cited as major issues. The fact that medical tourism depends heavily on private medical institutions aggravates existing healthcare inequalities and encourages a brain drain from public to private hospitals (Horowitz & Rosensweig, 2007).

Globalization and neo–liberalism have created favourable conditions for the increase of medical tourism, and Turkey's healthcare sector has experienced privatization and commercialization since the late 1980s. The revenue from medical tourism has increased considerably in the past few years. Medical tourists come mostly from Arab countries, the former Soviet Union and Balkan countries, and most recently European and American patients have started to choose Turkey for their treatment (Turkey's Ministry of Health Report, 2012). Considering the potential of this highly profitable global market, the Ministry of Health has developed new plans and regulations in accordance with its aspirations for the future of medical tourism, and the government is exploring new ways to facilitate patient access. For instance, Turkish Airlines, the national airline, offers a 10% price reduction for non–Turkish patients who travel to Turkey for medical purposes.

In 2010, Turkey's Ministry of Health issued a plan with a target of welcoming one million foreign patients by 2020. In line with this 10-year plan, eight cities have been designated for medical tourism. Major private hospitals in more economically developed cities such as Istanbul, Antalya, Izmir and Bursa are keen to cooperate with the Ministry, having a more developed bureaucratic infrastructure than most other Turkish hospitals. A rapid increase in the number of private hospitals has led to fierce competition. In order to attract more foreign patients, private hospitals import the latest medical technology in diagnostics and treatment, especially in robotic and laser surgery, and regularly send their doctors and nurses to Western countries for training in the latest diagnosis and treatment methods. Some of these hospitals also establish partnerships with or receive accreditations from prestigious foreign medical institutions. Some have opened liaison offices in the countries where they attract the most patients, while others send coordinators abroad regularly for promotional activities.

Medical tourism is a relatively new tourism product for Turkey, and rapid development has been facilitated by its established health system and new technology, the availability of qualified human resources, its geographic and cultural proximity to the main markets, and an established tourism infrastructure to provide complimentary services. Turkey has many state-of-the-art healthcare facilities, 51 of which are accredited by Joint Commission International (JCI). Between the years 2000 and 2005, the number of private hospitals in Turkey increased by 100%, and although the rate of increase has slowed, their numbers are still growing (Turkey's Ministry of Health web page). Physicians and other healthcare professionals in leading healthcare facilities are highly skilled and most of the physicians have substantial experience in international medical practices. In addition, Turkey enjoys the advantage of its central geographical location and transportation facilities. It is only a short flight from many cities in Europe, Central Asia and the Middle East. The prices of many medical procedures, operations and treatments are relatively cheaper compared to those in developed countries.

On the government side, medical tourism has also drawn considerable attention. Turkey's Tourism Strategy 2023 is a master plan seeking to increase tourism to 50 million arrivals by 2023 and to expand the tourism economy to US$86 billion. The goal is to establish Turkey as a world brand in tourism and to place it in the top five receiving countries. The plan identifies nine tourism development areas, seven thematic tourism corridors, ten tourism cities and five eco–tourism zones and encourages investment by public sector interventions, with medical tourism for overseas visitors as a priority. Page (2009, p.426) notes that "this is a massive expansionist programme for a destination that has already faced numerous problems linked with tourism. It is also somewhat surprising to find such an expansionist strategy when many other countries" are struggling with the effects of travel and tourism on climate change. This raises issues for the way in which tourism is embraced as a development option as well as for the way it spreads, and for controlling problems of growth.

This chapter focuses only on the area of medical tourism that includes medical procedures requiring the services of a qualified physician. An estimated 270,000 people visited Turkey for healthcare tourism purposes in 2011 (Turkey's Ministry of Health Medical Tourism Assessment Report, 2012). Turkey has become an important medical tourism destination, currently hosting more than 40,000 foreign medical tourists, and has only recently started to activate its potential (Erdogan & Yilmaz, 2012). According to the Medical Tourism Assessment Report (2012), the main challenges for business sustainability seem to be the need for more professional integration of the organizations active in the healthcare tourism market, and lack of reliable statistical data and methods to increase the share of governmental organizations in medical tourism, which is about 27%. Yet other challenges lurking on the horizon are environmental and societal sustainability concerns, given that medical tourism impacts these areas in terms of an increase in the amount of hazardous medical waste that may impinge on local communities' access to health services (Bristow, 2008).

The purpose of this chapter is to report and discuss the results of our investigation on whether sustainability is taken as a dimension while developing the medical tourism product and managing the related processes in Turkey. Although there are a few pieces of exploratory research on the state of medical tourism in Turkey, the sustainability dimension of the issue remains untouched. Three objectives were identified in this chapter to accomplish the following goals: assessment of the situation of medical tourism in Turkey from a sustainability perspective, identification of how organizations with a focus on medical tourism providing service for international patients in Istanbul treat sustainability, and proposals for a more sustainable way of managing medical tourism.

10.2. Literature Review

Medical tourism appeared on the global stage in the days of classical Greece. Pilgrims used to travel from various places throughout the Mediterranean to a small territory in the Saronic Gulf called Epidauria, which was known as the healing place (Gahlinger, 2008). In the recent past, the direction of medical tourism was from the developing countries to the developed to be able to get treatments that were not available in the home country. In the last decades, medical tourism, that is, combining medical interventions with tourism facilities, is a growing sector in several developing countries, mostly in the Far East and South America (Mechinda *et al.*, 2010). Current developments in information technology have accelerated this trend because these developments allow people to make comparisons and choices.

From ancient times onwards, the search for treatment has been a motivation for travelling. Although the scale of medical travel and its commercial volume have changed dramatically, the essential motivation remains the same. Today people are still moving from one country to another in search of medical care. Scholars and practitioners have each provided their own definitions for medical tourism. According to Lee and Spisto (2007, p.2), medical tourism is "a travel activity that involves a medical procedure or activities that promote the well-being of the tourist". Bookman and Bookman (2007, p.1) define medical tourism as "an economic activity that entails trade in services and represents the splicing of at least two sectors: medicine and tourism".

Medical treatments can be grouped into two main categories. The first includes treatments that are administered by qualified practitioners or physicians. The second comprises treatments offered by health professionals who are registered and recognized by a local health institution as qualified providers of wellness services. As noted by Fuchs and Reichel (2010, p.207), although the terms health, medical and wellness tourism are often used interchangeably in the tourism literature, it is certainly more useful to distinguish medical tourism as that involving specific "medical interventions with expected substantial and long-term outcomes". To separate medical tourism and other forms of health tourism such as SPA and wellness tourism, Dawn and Pal's (2011) definition for medical tourism as the act of travelling to other countries to obtain medical, dental and surgical care, could also be useful.

Various factors influence the choice of a medical tourism destination. In Smith and Forgione's (2007) study, these factors are categorized into two phases: the choice of a destination, and the choice of an international medical facility. The first phase involves external factors, which include economic conditions, political climate, social behaviour and regulatory standards. In essence, potential patients are more likely to choose destinations where healthcare is a high priority in the host country, where they can feel welcomed by the local community, and where patient protection provisions are similar to those in their home country.

Palvia (2007) identifies costs, accreditation, quality of care and physicians' training as determinant factors. For example, in the case of American patients, cost can be a major factor because the treatment they receive in their country can be up to 10 times as expensive as the treatment that they could receive in the host country. In addition to cost, accreditations and quality of care can play a role. Organizational documents such as JCI accreditation are often used by patients and patient sending agencies in deciding the destination. The last factor, physicians' training, refers to the extensiveness of the training an institution gives to its medical staff. Through their empirical work, Mechinda and colleagues (2010) showed that satisfaction and trust are among the key factors in the attitudinal loyalty of medical tourists.

As an emerging market economy, Turkey experienced a boom in the last few years in terms of investment in medical care (TUSIAD, 2009). During the last four years, hospital patient numbers have steadily increased, with a large share of the increase in private hospitals as a result of changes in legislation. The increase is expected to have effects on different dimensions. Private hospitals took the lead in the medical tourism field, and then the responsible public institutions – namely the Ministries of Health, Economy, and Culture and Tourism – started to institutionalize it and position it within a certain framework to facilitate development in line with the expectations of private entrepreneurs, who were already leading actors in the sector. From a business perspective of sustainability, Lee (2006) regards medical tourism as a more sustainable form of tourism because there is an ongoing demand for affordable healthcare from Europe and often for luxury from the Middle East. He suggests that governments generally support medical tourism, as it is a high value product providing foreign capital. Government support is important in the development of medical tourism, as new visa arrangements, for example, might be needed for special treatments. It is also an indication of quality and confidence.

Even at this relatively early stage, medical tourism's viability as a tool for sustainable development should be questioned. Sustainability is not new for many healthcare organizations. For years they have been planning how to better manage the resources they consume and how to serve the local community as a natural part of their business operations. In general, the longer an organization has been operating, the greater the value they assign to sustainability. What is new is the way they think about the triple bottom line (people, profit and planet) and moving from an informal approach to a more formal and structured approach. According to Hart and Milstein (2003), a sustainable medical facility has the following four targets: 1) building a strong foundation and addressing environmental issues, 2) improving community relations, 3) the expansion of services offered, and 4) gaining patients from new markets.

Sustainability could be an important criterion from a traveller's point of view as well. The results of Innman's survey (cited in Mechinda *et al.*, 2010) suggest that medical tourists are cost sensitive and want good quality, yet are aware of the needs of local workers. Although the care of the patient should always come first, the local community should not be at a disadvantage simply because they cannot afford the attention that foreign medical tourists demand (see Table 10.1). Sustainable practices can also be used not only to increase the quality but also the quantity of the service. Erdogan and Yilmaz (2010) suggest that with sustainable management principles, Turkey can become a stronger competitor in the sector.

Connell (2005) argues that economic benefits, employment opportunities and reversing the brain drain are expected advantages of the process. However, another drain can occur in the public sector in terms of skilled health workers moving to the private sector, increasing the burden on the public sector and putting forward ethical issues, including equity and competitive involvement questions. For example, in Thailand a doctor in the private sector can earn in one day the equivalent of a week's salary in the public sector. Under these circumstances, more skilled surgeons and doctors find positions in private hospitals that cater for more affluent patients while the public system offers health care for low-cost medical operations. The other question is related to the environmental aspect of the issue. According to the World Health Organization, 20% of the waste which is generated poses a danger to health. This is a very important issue for Costa Rica, where the hospitals produce tons of waste, 25% of which is labelled as bio–hazardous, according to Bristow, Yang and Lu (2011). They examine the issue also from the social perspective of medical tourism and address questions on this issue for Costa Rica. The question is whether the local people who live near eco-medical facilities are able to have access to healthcare or not, because of the raised prices of medical care. To sum up, medical tourism should be embraced with its advantages – bearing in mind the negative effects, for which remedies should be sought. In this context, it is beneficial to understand the point of view of medical tourism centres on three pillars of sustainability (see Table 10.1).

Table 10.1 – The Three Pillars of Sustainability

Business sustainability	Social sustainability	Environmental sustainability
Sustainability management system	Contribution to the development of local community	Energy consumption
Periodic guidance and sustainability training for personnel	Access of local community to the activities of the organization	Water consumption
Measurement of customer satisfaction, including sustainability aspects	Human resources policies	Waste management
Sustainability claims in promotional materials	Familiarization of medical tourists with the local community	Purchasing policies

10.3. Methodology

The study aimed to determine how organizations in Istanbul with a medical tourism focus treat sustainability. Using an adaptation of the Global Sustainable Tourism Council performance indicators, a semi-structured survey was conducted in order to obtain a deeper understanding on the views of sustainability. As private enterprises dominate the sector, a judgmental sampling of the hospitals and clinics with enough substitutes was composed from the membership list of the Turkish Healthcare Travel Council, the leading umbrella organization for medical tourism in Turkey. The selected institutions were targeted to scrutinize whether sustainability is a criterion for their incentives dedicated to medical tourism investments.

Eight semi-structured interviews of approximately 30–45 minutes each were conducted addressing managers of private hospitals and clinics involved in medical tourism. Five of the institutions were general hospitals and three were clinics and a specialized hospital. The people interviewed were international marketing, quality management and/or international relations directors. The interviews were conducted in person, and were audio recorded. Hand-written notes were taken throughout the interview. The survey addressed the demographic data of the hospitals and their sustainability practices. Probing questions were used to identify further insights. When necessary, explanations were provided on notions such as business sustainability, as the concept seemed new for some interviewees.

The data was analysed using the thematic content analysis method and through presenting the themes that emerged from the interviews. Several steps were taken in the data analysis. The first step was transcribing all the interviews, deductive coding of the transcripts followed by inductive coding, and narrowing down the data by eliminating irrelevant information. The second step was creating a list of thematic codes. The third step was merging and refining the relevant codes to meaningful themes. After a series of discussions, the final codes were established.

The limitations of this research were largely parallel to those of other studies. This study was designed as a descriptive assessment of medical tourism and its sustainable management practices in Istanbul, but due to the large number of health organizations in the city, the sample size was bound to be modest. Today around 40% of private hospitals are situated in Istanbul, and on the one hand, this provided the opportunity to reach a fair approximation for the country. Another constraint that could have had an impact on the results was that all of the interviewees were from private health organizations. Although the vast majority of medical tourism activity in Turkey has been realized by private health organizations, this may have prompted a more managerial perspective on the issue.

10.4. Results

The officials of the hospitals and clinics that we interviewed were in private organizations that had been engaged in medical tourism activities for the last eight years, with special staff assigned for medical tourists. An important finding of the present investigation is that the economic gain seems to be higher in general hospitals compared with clinics. Hospital officials reported earning more income with fewer patients because the reason for the visits is often for more complicated and expensive treatments such as cancer and organ transplantation. As such, these hospitals do not see tourism as part of their ordinary activity but as a distinct business, while clinics try to engage patients through packages. According to the interviewees, in the global medical tourism market, Turkey positions itself with both its price and technology. While citizens of developing countries prefer Turkey for its technology, price is a stronger factor for travellers from more developed countries. The countries of origin are related to cultural proximity: Balkan countries, European countries, Middle Eastern countries and Turkic republics. Cultural proximity can explain this categorization, as some interviewees indicated. As the list of source countries suggests, Turkey attracts tourists partly due to its ease of accessibility. The extensive network and high quality image of Turkish Airlines (THY) was perceived to be a determiner in this case. Turkish Airlines' global network is a factor which makes Turkey more accessible and a more popular destination in return. Turkish Airlines provides a support package for patients who travel to Turkey for medical tourism and has had protocols with several healthcare organizations since 2009 (healthinturkey.org). This provides the medical facilities in Istanbul with a clear advantage, as Istanbul is the main hub of THY.

10.4.1. Business sustainability

In the interviews, the first question, "do you have a sustainability management system?" proved to be incomprehensible to most of the interviewees, because sustainability is not understood as something to be managed and assessed within a system. As the term "sustainability" was not clear for most of the interviewees, different aspects of a business are evoked in the minds of the interviewees and quality is perceived as the equivalent for business sustainability. However, this does not mean that these institutions do not have any activities that foster sustainability. Hospitals tend to secure accreditations from such agencies as JCI or TEMOS to increase their quality. In addition to accreditation, customer satisfaction is measured, assessed and actions are taken for the sustainability of the business. Image is an important factor in destination choice. According to the interviewees, while Turkey is in a good position, it should still be improved. Hospitals carry out many activities under different departments such as international marketing, quality management, patient relations and corporate communication. There are some activities carried out for various purposes contributing to the sustainability of these processes, but they do not measure and assess their sustainability. There is no such notion as promoting the hospital/clinic as a sustainable one. Finally, cooperation between the public and private sectors seems to play a key role in the development of medical tourism. Agreements between ministries and incentives offered by the state are said to be very influential in the development of this business. The respondents also emphasized the need for cooperation within the country and for investment in image–making.

10.4.2. Social sustainability

One of the benefits of medical tourism for the local community is the economic development that medical centres are creating. Medical centres put forward the idea that medical tourism and/or their institution creates a multiplier effect and brings economic development to the local community and the country. Although interviewees frequently emphasized the multiplier effect, there are no reliable statistics showing that local people are really employed and enjoying the economic benefits that the institutions are creating. The rise of medical tourism encourages the privatization of health care. As Connell (2005) suggests, this situation causes a brain drain in the public service all over the world. Access to skilled doctors can be difficult to attain for local patients who cannot afford treatment in a private institution. For example, although there is a boom in medical tourism in India, 40% of India's population live below the poverty line and have no access to even basic health care, and infant and maternal mortality rates are high. In Turkey, the human resources for the private hospitals are mainly provided by public hospitals, as stated by the interviewees. The occupational health and security of employees is sustained within the legal framework but it does not indicate that there will not be further brain drain in the public service. On the positive side, expertise and knowledge are shared free of charge through social responsibility projects with the general public in Turkey, and in some cases, abroad. Some hospitals sponsor activities such as sports. One hospital, through links with hospitals abroad, shares and discusses practices between hospitals. Although the health organizations investigated are organizing corporate social responsibility (CSR) activities, there is no clear information that they are not "green washing" and that the local community is really benefiting. From the patients' point of view, it is also important to be able to familiarize themselves with the local community. As many foreign patients seek information regarding their treatment on a regular basis, health organizations have established specific departments that help foreign patients with their medical trips from their arrival through to their departure.

10.4.3. Environmental sustainability

While hospitals create a great capacity to heal, the healthcare industry is a sizable consumer of natural resources. Medical waste is a worldwide environmental burden and 20% of the waste generated from healthcare facilities is hazardous (World Health Organisation, 2011). In the eyes of the interviewees, the primary stakeholder in environmental issues seems to be municipalities, as most of the interviewees stated that waste management is regulated by legislation and accreditation systems. Accordingly, the accumulated waste is parsed by source, and its treatment is outsourced to municipalities and, in some cases, to professional companies. Most of the time, waste management and energy efficiency are associated with "cost"; in other words, these activities are conducted simply to decrease costs. According to the interviewees, ecological and local products are not necessarily preferred. Purchasing policies are defined according to price, quality and safety standards. In a nutshell, it is hard to claim that the hospitals and clinics investigated are concerned primarily with environmental sustainability.

10.5. Conclusion

In Turkey, the efforts of the Ministries of Health and Culture and Tourism to develop medical tourism have not remained at the facilitation level but have turned instead to provision of incentives. Seizing the opportunity, medical tourism projects for public hospitals have been developed by the ministries. Yet the largest percentage (73%) of medical treatment for foreigners is provided by private enterprises (Ministry of Health Medical Tourism Assessment Report, 2012). The harsh competition in the sector pushes small clinics to combine tourism values with medical services. General hospitals do not often engage in the preparation of packages, while clinics turn to packages to make a difference. As one of the interviewees puts it, "Packages are used mostly by small clinics and plastic surgery. Big hospitals like us don't engage in such business".

Accreditation is widely sought among medical institutions. The accreditation can be sourced from different countries such as the USA (e.g., JCI) or from Germany (e.g., TEMOS). The main motivation for gaining accreditation is to reach new market segments and to assure potential patients that the medical facility is as viable an alternative as the ones in their own country. Affiliations with external organizations are often utilized and advertised online to attract potential medical tourists. These external organizations can be tourism stakeholders such as tourism agencies or foreign governmental agencies. These kinds of collaborations are stated to be common. Moreover, there is a general agreement that, due to its central position, a positive tourism image and strong logistics are advantages for Turkey, as it is easily accessible from other regions.

Another characteristic of the health sector is patient affairs. As many patients need guidance and information before and after their operations, private medical facilities have established specific departments to help and direct patients from their arrival at the airport. Hospitals and clinics also pay attention to the credentials of their medical staff. Skilled physicians are selected with great care and are often transferred from the public sector by private sector organizations. As part of their public relations, social responsibility campaigns initiated by medical facilities are often stated by the institutions. However, although social sustainability constitutes an important aspect of the institutions' policies, whether or not the local community benefits of these has not been reliably measured. The multiplier effect is stated as the most important social benefit but, again, it is not clear who is benefiting from the economic gain.

The study revealed that sustainability is generally associated with quality of management and related to accreditation systems. This was mainly because sustainability management is not yet an established tool applied in medical tourism development. The sustainability of the business is understood as the main objective, but there are other activities realized in the name of other purposes which are actually contributing to sustainability. Medical tourism is a growing sector where the primary motivations of the patients are low prices, high technology, good quality and quick access to medical centres. Like any other sector, it generates both positive and negative impacts on society, the economy and the environment. Sustainable development can be achieved in medical tourism if the three pillars of sustainability are considered along the entire service chain. All stakeholders should be made aware of the importance of social, economic and environmental sustainability. To these ends, the recommendations below are developed.

Establishing an Organization for Developing a Medical Accreditation System for Turkey: Holding a medical accreditation from the JCI means spending more than US$10,000 each quarter for medical facilities, which contributes to cost increases for medical treatments for foreign patients (Harryono, Huang, Miyazawa & Sethaput, 2006). For this reason, medical tourism establishments in Turkey should found an accreditation body that can replace foreign accreditation organizations. As a result, medical tourism facilities would not be required to pay large sums of money for accreditation. Instead, a local organization could receive an annual fee from each facility and elevate the medical services so that they are in line with/to the level of international medical standards and regulations. The benefit of this network would be to save money by not relying on foreign international accreditation organizations or insurance companies. Another benefit of this organization would be the provision of a control mechanism for small clinics, as it is currently very difficult for potential patients to understand the quality of service in clinics.

Creating a Medical Tourism Network with Direct Governmental Collaboration: The Government of Turkey can establish direct collaborations with a medical tourism network. Without direct participation from the government, the medical tourism network will not have the power to implement legislation to eliminate the risk of wrong-doing among medical tourism facilities. Creating a law for malpractice would motivate medical facilities to purchase malpractice insurance. The

Ministry of Health and the Ministry of Culture and Tourism could collaborate by assigning objectives within the national tourism strategy for enhancing medical tourism. A marketing strategy should be developed to enhance Turkey's image by cooperating with tourism operators and governmental offices around the world to promote medical tourism as one entity. Additionally, incentives can be offered according to sustainability parameters defined by the network.

Increasing the Environmental Sustainability Control of Municipalities: The addressees of the environmental concerns of health organizations are often the municipalities. For environmental practices, most of the hospitals use municipality services for waste management. The hospitals parse the waste in place and hand it over to the municipality. Giving training on environmental sustainability to the department responsible for waste management in the municipality can contribute to the processes and decision making regarding the handling of waste being collected from hospitals. Moreover, increasing the legal control of the municipalities over the health organizations could help to improve environmental sustainability.

Marketing Sustainability: A well-planned marketing strategy can lead organizations to gain a better competitive advantage. Such a strategy could be developed in collaboration with governmental agencies and umbrella institutions of health organizations. Awareness could be generated on the notion that sustainability can be a determiner in the choice of the destination for tourists, especially those coming from major European countries. A sustainability-integrated marketing strategy can also encourage other medical facilities to bring sustainability onto their agenda.

Corporate Social Responsibility Activities: These activities seem to be undefined and left to the initiative of individual institutions. An alternative could be the development of CSR regulations by the government, such as setting medical capacity for local patients. As hospitals aim to attract more foreign tourists, they may ignore the needs of local patients. With a defined capacity maintained to host local patients, social responsibility initiatives can be more structured.

The research reported in this chapter aimed to understand how viable sustainability is as a dimension of medical tourism and how it is practiced in the Istanbul health organizations which include medical tourism on their agendas. For those who are willing to expand knowledge and contribute to this field of study, future research on developing a sustainable medical facility framework or defining stakeholders in medical tourism and their roles can be useful areas of further investigation.

Acknowledgments

We would like to thank to the interviewees for their valuable time, and acknowledge Oznur Kotbas's contribution in this chapter's reported study, at an earlier phase. The study was partially supported by the Institute of Social Sciences and the Department of Tourism Administration, Bogazici University, Turkey.

References

Bookman, M.Z., & Bookman, K.R. (2007). *Medical tourism in developing countries*. New York: Palgrave Macmillan.

Bristow, R.S. (2008) Eco-medical tourism: Can it be sustainable? *Proceedings of the 2008 Northeastern Recreation Research Symposium*, 158-164.

Bristow, R.S., Yang, W-T., & Lu, M-T. (2011). Sustainable medical tourism in Costa Rica: Health and medical tourism. *Tourism Review*, 66(1/2), 107-117.

Connell, J. (2005). Medical tourism: Sea, sun, sand and . . . surgery. *Tourism Management*, 27, 1093–1100.

Dawn, D., & Pal, S. (2011). Medical tourism in India: Issues, opportunities, and designing strategies for growth and development. *International Journal of Multidisciplinary Research*, 1(3), 185-202.

Erdogan, S., & Yilmaz, E. (2012). Medical tourism: An assessment on Turkey. *Proceedings of the 10th International Conference on Knowledge, Economy and Management*.

Fuchs, G., & Reichel, A. (2010). Health tourists visiting a highly volatile destination, *Anatolia: An International Journal of Tourism and Hospitality Research*, 21, 205-225.

Gahlinger, P. (2008). The medical tourism travel guide: Your complete reference to top-quality, low-cost dental, cosmetic, medical care & surgery overseas. *Sunrise River Press*.

Harryono, M., Huang, Y.-F., Miyazawa, K., & Sethaput, V. (2006). *Thailand Medical Tourism Cluster*. Thailand: Harvard Business School.

Hart, S.L., & Milstein, M.B. (2003). Creating sustainable value. *Academy of Management Executive*, 17, 56-69.

healthinturkey.org. Turkish Airlines Medical Tourism Support Package. Available at: http://www.healthinturkey.org/en-EN/news--events/7_turkish-airlines-medical-tourism-support-package.aspx. Accessed October 6, 2014.

Horowitz, M., & Rosensweig, J. (2007). Medical tourism: Globalization of the healthcare marketplace, *Journal of Medscape General Medicine*, 9, 33-49.

Lee, C. (2006). Medical tourism, an innovative opportunity for entrepreneurs, *Journal of Asia Entrepreneurship and Sustainability*, 3(1), 110-123.

Lee, C., & Spisto, M. (2007). Medical tourism: The future of health services. 12th International Conference on ISO 9000 and TQM, 1-7. Taichung.

Mechinda, P., Serirat, S., Anuwichanont, J., & Gulid, N. (2010), An examination of tourists' loyalty towards medical tourism in Pattaya, Thailand, *The International Business and Economics Research Journal*, 9, 55-70.

Page, S. (2009). *Tourism Management: Managing for Change*. Slovenia: Elsevier.

Palvia, S. (2007). *Global Outsourcing of IT and IT Enabled Services: a Relationship Framework and Two Stage Model for Selecting a Vedor*. Ivy League Publishing.

Smith, P. C., & Forgione, D. A. (2007). Global outsourcing of healthcare: A medical tourism decision model. *Journal of IT Case and Application Research*, 9(3), 19.

Turkey's Ministry of Health web page. Tourism and health. http://www.saglik.gov.tr/SaglikTurizmi/belge/1-10592/turizm-ve-saglik.html. Accessed October 7, 2014.

Turkey's Ministry of Health Medical Tourism Report (2012). http://ilegra.com.tr/saglikturizmi/dokumanlar/degerlendirme-raporu.pdf. Downloaded October 17, 2014.

TUSIAD (2009).Turkiye icin yeni bir firsat penceresi: Tip turizmi gorus belgesi: Available at: http://www.tusiad.org.tr/_rsc/shared/file/tip-turizmi-baski-SON-Aralik-2009.pdf. Accessed March 7, 2014.

World Health Organization (2014). Waste from Healthcare Activities. Available at http://www.who.int/mediacentre/factsheets/fs253/en/. Accessed October 2.

CHAPTER ELEVEN

THE COASTAL AREA AS A TOURIST SCENARIO: THE CASE OF VILLA GESELL

GRACIELA BENSENY

Abstract

In the late nineteenth century, on the coast of the province of Buenos Aires (Argentina) the city of Mar del Plata is positioned as the premier tourist destination of sun and beach. The success achieved encourages and promotes the development of new coastal urbanizations; emerging small seaside resorts that impose a new model of territorial organization. This chapter discusses the importance of coastal areas as a resource and scenario in the evolution of Villa Gesell where applying the geo-historical method the urbanization process and the impact on the environment is investigated. **Keywords:** tourist urbanization, tourism development, environmental trouble, coastal areas, Argentina.

11.1. Introduction

The sun and beach tourism in the Province of Buenos Aires becomes important with the foundation of Mar del Plata (1874). Its positioning as a holiday destination, together with the enhancement of the coastal edge of large "estancias" (farms) for urban purposes, led to the emergence of different resorts located in the vicinity and a new territorial occupancy model, understood as how to occupy and transform the space, incorporating different uses to the existing ones and beginning a process that will leave its anthropization footprint on the environment.

In the late nineteenth century resorts located south of Mar del Plata arise: Necochea (1881), Miramar (1888) and Mar del Sud (1889); whereas the following century fosters the development of tourist resorts located north: Ostende (1908), Villa Gesell (1931), Mar de Ajo (1934), San

Clemente del Tuyú (1935), San Bernardo (1943), Pinamar (1943), among others.

In the new spaces created, tourism becomes the driving shaft of the local economy and the organization is the result of multiple interrelations between society and nature. The coastal zone is valued and quickly transformed into an urban space where new urban-tourist uses compete with the already existing agricultural livestock operations. New beach resorts try to imitate and replicate European urban models, originated for the enjoyment of the ruling elite, and then some of those transformed into mass destinations, reproducing the features of uniformity imposed by the development of sun and beach tourism.

In particular, the town of Villa Gesell is selected as the unit of study and it presents some results of the thesis "The coastal area as a tourist scenario. The case of Villa Gesell (Argentina)", defended and evaluated at the Southern National University (Argentina), where the importance of the coastal area as a resource and scenario in the evolution of tourism developments is analyzed. Through geo-historical method, urbanization and consequences of tourism in the coastal zone which generates a complex environmental problem is investigated.

Villa Gesell is located at 37° 22' South latitude and 02' 57th West longitude. It has temperate oceanic climate, with average temperatures of 22°C (January) and 8°C (July), sits on a dune barrier width varying between 3 and 5 km., and has low sedimentary shores. It has an area of 28,500 hectares, which comprises the towns of Villa Gesell, Las Gaviotas, Mar de las Pampas and Mar Azul. According to the latest census conducted by the National Institute of Statistics and Census 2010, the stable population includes 31,353 people (15,750 men and 15,603 women).

Villa Gesell integrates Buenos Aires Atlantic Tourist Corridor, comprised of the following towns: La Costa, Pinamar, Villa Gesell, Mar Chiquita, General Pueyrredon (Mar del Plata) and General Alvarado (Miramar), linked by the Provincial Route 11. Each location of the tourist corridor tries to differentiate and supplement during the summer months, acting as centres of stay and/or distribution, and disputing national tourism demand. The mature tourist destinations are Mar del Plata and Miramar, whereas the rest of the towns arise in the mid-twentieth century.

Villa Gesell is a specialized sun and beach tourist centre, with strong sales activity during the summer and construction during the rest of the year. According to data supplied by the Ministry of Tourism, tourism demand reach over a million visitors a year, with the highest concentrations during the summer period, followed by the long weekend of October 12 where historically the "Week of the race" or "Diversity" is celebrated. Villa Gesell is one of the main beaches and tourist attraction centre with national affluence.

The history of Villa Gesell is linked to the figure of its founder Carlos Gesell, businessman originally dedicated to the manufacture and sale of furniture and baby articles, who in 1931 decided to plant a forest in a wide field of dunes, and thus ensure the obtaining the raw material for his industry (Gesell, 1983). Its history reflects the opportunity to purchase a large field at a low price, followed by a strong intervention and transforming action of the natural resource, which implied substantial monetary investment and a change in his business direction, resulting the wood in a complex urbanization that grows without proper planning that creates serious environmental problems.

11.2. Literature Review

In the words of Barrado and Calabuig (2001), the coastal area represents the geographic area of transition between the continent (coastal area) and ground water (submerged litoral zone). It is a very dynamic interface area where there is a strong relationship between terrestrial and marine ecosystems. It combines the heterogeneity of the coast (morphology, topography, climate, vegetation, habitat) and the value provided by the submerged zone, the sea being the integrating element of the coastal landscape. It constitutes a high calling and a favourite tourist flow scenario with different scale and magnitude.

From a geographic perspective, tourism in the coastal area involves the consumption of natural resources and their transformation into a leisure area where the motionless location of natural resources generates the need for on-site consumption and motivates the movement of people. The favourable natural conditions of landscape combined by the sea and the beach, make the geophysical resource that fosters the development of sun and beach tourism, whose equipment and infrastructure works made by man are added to provide greater attractiveness to the coastal space.

From the point of view of tourism, coastal resources form a recreational space for helium practices and sports, in a very dynamic area, where there is a strong relationship between terrestrial and marine ecosystems. In the words of Vera Rebollo et al. (1997), the presence of natural resources defines the spatial location of tourism and this allows to differentiate the tourist function configured by the environment.

Tourism in the coastal zone implies a high consumption of land, which associated with the tourist-recreational practices and models of urbanization, produce changes in the territorial, social and economic structures. Traditional activities give way to models of implementation imposed by tourism, urbanization accelerates and configures tourism specialization. According to Vera Rebollo *et al.* (1997, p.93), "urban-tourism becomes the polarizer and dynamic factor in local economies of the coast and its expansion is contingent on the possibilities and land availability (reduced agricultural interest, proximity to the sea), market opportunities (demand growth) and infrastructure development".

The coastal area is fragile and presents high vulnerability to infrastructure works and tourism infrastructure. As contemporary authors specialized in geography literature (Strahler & Strahler, 2005) and geography of tourism (Callizo-Soñeiro, 1991; Lozato-Giotart, 1990; Pearce, 1988; Vera Rebollo *et al.*, 1997), say the tourism development of coastline land requires a thorough knowledge of the ecosystem, as works made by man may modify or alter the ecological balance and natural resource can be damaged. The creation of an artificial coastline with buildings on the sand, piers or elements that act as a windbreak, commercial marinas works modify coastal dynamics, impact and alter the natural landscape, causing alterations that resent the dynamics of the coastal area and consequently the environmental balance.

The coastal areas are key elements of the tourism network in constant and complex restructuring, and in turn play a key role in relation to their contribution as recipients of domestic tourist destinations mainly, as well as to the development at local and regional level, without forgetting the stress generated at the territorial level and uncertainty about their future.

11.3. Methodology

Under an exploratory and descriptive study environmental problems that arise from the different territorial transformations in Villa Gesell, with the aim of analyzing the works in the coastal zone during the process of appropriation of the territory, the future of research and beaches management of coastal areas implemented by the municipality are investigated, through consulting literature and interviewing different stakeholders. The application of the geo-historical method defines three periods: a) dune fixation, b) foundation and social formation, c) tourist consolidation, analyzing the variables: natural resource transformation, exploitation of the coastal zone, equipment and infrastructure tourist works on the beach and role of stakeholders, allowing to understand the environmental consequences of tourist real-estate development and reflect upon the presence or absence of a proper management of coastal areas.

To make this study, National Population Census (1980/2010 period), catastral maps (available at Municipal Archive Museum Villa Gesell), documentation and printed newspapers, online information sites, municipal ordinances and development plans are analyzed. The sources of data collection are based on visits by direct observation (2006/2012 period in different seasons), semi-structured interviews to public sector leaders (Director of Tourism, Secretary of Planning, Coordinator of Environmental Area); private tourism sector (Chamber of Real Estate, Association of Hotels, Restaurants, Confectionery and Allied Villa Gesell, Chamber of Commerce, Chamber of Public Tourist Beach Units of Villa Gesell) and representatives of the third sector with tourism-related environmental issues (Environmental Association Verdemar, In defense of the Coastal Dune).

The consultation of documentary and virtual sources and the data gathered during the field work, provide insight into the historical development of the town, through the environmental analysis, the network of settlements, morphology of the plot, mode of land occupation urban expansion and functional organization (primary economic activities, secondary, tertiary). By comparing plans that respond to different historical moments, the information collected during the interviews and consulted on information sites, form of ownership of land and its impact on the environment is analyzed. It is expected that the research results will help raise awareness among managers and the community about the importance of conserving the natural resource and environmental criteria prevailing over economic decision-making.

11.4. Results

The tourist development of Villa Gesell arises in three historical moments, where the transformation of natural resources, the exploitation of the coastal zone, equipment construction and tourist infrastructure on the beach and role of stakeholders are analyzed. The first session focuses on dune fixation (1931-1940), the second analyzes the foundation and social formation (1941-1970), based on colonization and finding investors to form a new company and the third aims to tourism consolidation through the development of the village added to the value given to the beach as a natural and economic resource (1971-2012).

a) Dune fixation: 1931–1940

The history of the city begins in 1931 with the acquisition of Carlos Gesell of public land (1,648 has. of dunes), located in the Municipality of General Madariaga, due to a readjustment of measurement of the maritime border of the "estancia" of the Leloir family dedicated to the agricultural-livestock farm. After two failed real estate transactions (Sáenz Valiente born in Madariaga tries pigs breeding and Eduardo Credaro proposes industrial sand mining), Gesell sees the opportunity to plant a forest to ensure the raw material of his family business. In the words of Masor (1975, p.31) "the property was unproductive and hostile, a piece of desert nestled like a sentence in the General Madariaga, unspoilt and impermeable to progress". However, according to the story of the founder's daughter, his father was amazed by the extension of the beaches and the presence of dunes (Gesell, 1983).

The transformation of the natural resource begins with afforestation tasks with different exotic species, both domestic and foreign (Melilotus Alba, Myoporum Acuminatum, Acacias Trinervis, Saligna and Robinia), Australian Eucalyptus, Poplar Tamarisk (Adesmia Incana) and Esparto, which make the native flora capable of resisting soil conditions, water scarcity and deposition of marine salts on their leaves, the founder planted 120,000 locust trees on the southern slopes of the dunes (Gesell, 1983; Masor, 1975; Sierra, 1969).

The recovery of the coastal zone begins with the construction of two buildings (founder family and employees) and the transformation of natural resource by fixing dunes. Afforestation tasks valued the property and involved a heavy monetary investment that caused a family rift and removal of the business venture Carlos Gesell, now single landowner. The incipient forest became the origin of a new challenge, based on the decision to start a holiday resort.

The equipment and infrastructure works on the beach are reduced to shadow lying and the installation of a tent during the summer for family enjoyment (Gesell, 1983). In this historical period the only social actor is the owner, who makes all the decisions about the forest and the future tourism development.

b) Foundation and social formation: 1941–1970

The transformation of the natural resource by setting the dunes changed the original environmental conditions and favoured the development of urbanization. Gesell, builds a summer house to let (La Golondrina) and starts an urban-tourism project. Afforestation granted greater economic value to the property and new green spaces created by anthropic action became an attractive place.

The recovery of the coastal zone favours the development of urbanization, Gesell focuses on the foundation and finding strategies that encourage the arrival of settlers and investors to build a new society. In 1941 he takes a first subdivision 1,200 m distance from the coast, grid layout (600 m. 5 km., divided into 24 sections of 1 ha. each). The sales strategy encouraged mortgage the land in favour of the founder, with a ten-year repayment period; with an additional payment, the seller forests the plot with species transplanted from the nursery. The sales pitch left implicit future development that would reach the urbanization and the possibility of subdividing the acquired hectare in 20 plots.

During the summer of 1941 the first tourists entered the slogan "the beach resort that is recommended from friend to friend" arises, the myth of a new casual, austere and pluralistic beach opposed to Mar del Plata tourism based on elitism is created. (Bevacqua, 2002). A second subdivision (1942) covers three discontinuous fractions in the north.

Gesell designs a holiday resort that escapes the traditional checkerboard, taking a winding route of the dunes looking for the valleys, with subdivisions that try to respect the topography, higher than the streets, to respect the original construction irregularities. The streets parallel to the coast are called Avenues and Paseos the perpendicular ones, applying increasing numbers for easy identification. The complex adopts a longitudinal design, parallel to the coast, where the first three avenues are intended to concentrate buildings for the hosting service; Avenue 3 concentrates shops and homes of permanent residents are located beyond Avenue 3 and Avenue 1.

The first hotels and summer houses, are built with an architectural design that combines central European picturesque and colonial patterns. The first houses built in the north side were simple, with external rustic lime plaster, with wooden enclosures of axed Lapacho (shutters and doors), Lapacho wood trusses and roof tiles two or four waters with deep foundations and chained to prevent cracking of the walls, looking for a low cost durable housing construction (Bevacqua, 2002). Gesell tried to build an alpine village on the Atlantic coast.

In 1943 the opening of the path from Route 11 to Villa Gesell is passed, the first general store opens (Avenue 3 and Paseo 105) there are four houses with permanent residents, the "Playa Hotel" (Paseos 205 and 304) with twelve rooms opens. In 1945 the hotels La Gaviota and Colonial are added. The resort has fifteen family houses and the following year twenty-five houses, increasing the permanent population. The founder registers their venture under the name "Villa Gesell". In 1948 there are 110 houses and the following year 300. (Masor, 1975).

In the words of Palavecino and García (2007, p.26), "the first settlers were mostly European, although there were many "criollos" of General Madariaga. Spanish was the least spoken language in the incipient town. There were Germans, Swiss, Swedes, Austrians, Hungarians, Poles, Jews, Russians and a lot of Italians". The Eastern Europeans settled down in the North sector, Spanish and Italian specializing in hotel, restaurant and construction, on Avenue 3.

The third subdivision (1947) covers from Paseo 308 to Paseo 108 affects the waterfront and acts as a southern boundary of the development until mid–twentieth century. Population growth increases fivefold; in 1960 the population reaches 1,347 residents and 6,341 in 1970.

The equipment and infrastructure works on the beach show a higher consumption of coastal areas, with urban-tourism uses, keeping the dunes without construction. Summer accommodation establishments and resort dwellings predominate concentrated in the first three avenues parallel to the coast. On the beach resorts are the first constructions are made of wood, with stilt design allowing the passage of the sand. The privatization of public space starts and the beach becomes an economic resource. Every summer new beaches are added, with the highest concentration in the downtown area.

The identification of social actor refers to the founder figure; during this historical period the concentration of power and hegemony stands in the political leadership. The destination was born at the sole initiative of the founder, who became the sole owner, developer and financial agent of urbanization, exercising absolute control of the growing town. To attract investors and families willing to survive in the initial conditions of the development, Gesell attuned to the Fordist model, assumes the role of the welfare state: donates the land and builds the first school, medical room, pharmacy, grocery, generates and supplies the electricity, and provides transportation services with his truck trying to encourage the establishment of new population (Gesell, 1983).

In 1950 he creates the Electricity Cooperative, in 1954 there were 307 connections and 778 recorded in 1959 (Masor, 1975). In 1963 Telephone Cooperative is founded. In 1949 there is a police station, transformed into "subcomisaría" (1957). During this historical moment new institutions arise in the community, led and promoted by the founder himself.

c) Consolidation of tourism: 1971–2012

The third historical moment aspires to consolidate Villa Gesell as a tourist destination for sun and beach, attached to that value given to the beach as a natural and economic resource. The decade of the seventies has a time of crisis and change; it is a transitional stage characterized by events, emergence of new players, changes in institutional power, technical and legal body that promotes the emergence of a new judicial organization.

The conversion of natural resources is emphasized in both the coastal areas for tourism and the urban space. In 1971 the pavement comes, Villa Gesell records high rates of construction, more urban coverage and sealing of natural substrate. In 1980, the first bead of dunes in the central area (Paseo 303 to Paseo123) is decapitated, the Costanera Avenue is created and alters coastal dynamics favouring the process of erosion. To attract new investors Gesell implements the "Plan Galopante" favouring an effective occupation and construction, based on the 50% reduction in land value if the building ends within six months.

The middle section consolidates and extends southward parallel to the coastal areas, deepening the population growth in the West area, with establishment of stable population. There are new neighbouring towns, product of another founder, Mar de las Pampas, Las Gaviotas and Mar Azul. The town grows without planning to structure urban sprawl, provide public spaces and the provision of infrastructure. Urban growth intensified in the 300 m. the waterfront and in the downtown areas of the city on dune barrier. The floor area increased soil impermeability and consequently surface flows evacuate directly onto the beach.

Environmental problems sharpen due to: expansion of the tourist development, development of facilities and infrastructure to support recreational use, beheading of the first strand of dunes, waterproofing dunes, lack of water runoff, salt water intrusion into the drinking water, aquifer pollution, over-exploitation of the beach resort because of the presence of a greater number of resorts built with cement and marked coastal erosion especially in the downtown area, to alter the balance between the system of dunes and beach produced by urbanization. Negative effects reflect the trivialization of the coastal zone, a deterioration in the landscape and environmental quality, a situation that leads to the loss of values and lack of uniqueness, decorating the coastal landscape with a design similar to other coastal areas regardless of equipment the geographic location where you are.

The recovery of the coastal zone evidence strong consumption of coastal areas, tall buildings are constructed in the first avenues and coastal scenery is decorated with stiff cement work, struggling and competing for a greater number of floors. In the downtown area the buildings are concentrated on high, cast shadow cones on the beach, alter the atmosphere conditions and decrease heliophany period.

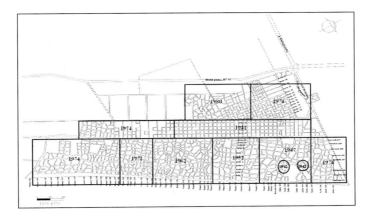

Figure 11.1 – Urban expansion Villa Gesell
Source: Own calculations based on published mapping in Tauber *et al.* 1998, p.29.

Equipment works and tourism infrastructure in the beach resorts propose replacing wood with new concrete buildings, which offer a wide range of services and facilities unrelated to the shadow units (pool, hairdresser, drugstore, telephone and fax, laundry, paddle tennis with concrete floors, parking, etc.). In 1996 there were 76 resorts, occupying an area of 21,000 m². all built with cement and competing for adding new services. One in five beach resorts offered public toilets, there was no water treatment, and management of quality service   and the environment was absent.

In this period there is strong pressure on the coastal zone, concentrated in the central area (Calle 303 / Paseo 129 Street). Urban sprawl leaves its mark on the beach, causes a gradual process of erosion affected by two Sudestadas (December 2003 and April 2004), which leaves behind a berm of 2 m. high and a strong decrease in the area of beach. To solve this problem the redevelopment of the waterfront (Municipal Ordinance 2050/06) was implemented based on: closing the Costanera Avenue, transfer pedestrian promenade toward the building line, reduction and relocation of beach resorts, new beach model (built with wood and on stilts), regeneration of the first cord of dunes between 107 and 109 Street, installing "enquinchados" and closing Streets (across to the coast) in the central area, becoming cul-de-sac (dead end streets) to reduce vehicular traffic and take pressure off the environment.

There are new social actors. The population is 6,341 inhabitants (1970) to 11,632 (1980). Population growth evidence the end of the hegemony of the founder and portends a change in the leadership of the development and definition of new roles among different socio-institutional actors, acting on a shared scenario and ideologically divided, where power is distributed and disputed among different sectors of the community.

In 1979 Carlos Gesell dies. Four years later the Party of Villa Gesell (Law N° 9949/83) is created from a process of territorial fragmentation of Party General Madariaga gestated by Decree Law N° 9024/78. The city has its own budget and authorities, manages municipal autonomy, plans urbanistic system and prioritizes public works investment.

The institutional sector is consolidated and private sector groups representing the main nucleating tourist services emerge: Association of Hotels, Restaurants, Confectionery and Allied Villa Gesell; Chamber of Commerce; Fiscal Tourist Units Villa Gesell Beach, Real Estate and House Chamber. The third sector is represented by the non-governmental organization called In Defence of Coastal Dune and the Environmental Association Verdemar.

11.5. Conclusion

Urbanization causes high pressure on the coastal zone, that along with tourist consolidation and increasing competition between maritime destinations in the province of Buenos Aires, intends to consider a change in driving destination that enables sustainability in the context of an integrated coastal management.

The beach as the main resource of the town changes its public character into private one becoming an economic resource, which over time develops different forms of use and activities. The rate of consumption marked by the tourist facilities of the beaches is imposed and with the passing of time becomes a destination that combines wood and concrete constructions, that cyclically alternate and try to harmonize with the environment.

The first resorts built with wood and located along the waterfront become modern and complex service systems, built with cement, increasing the number of shadow units from 1970. The 21st century introduced new ideas and a new perception of the beach as a resource and support of the economic activities of the town. A new remodelling process of the waterfront starts which responds to a political project focused on the recovery of the beach and a newly designed resort built of wood, on stilts, raised off the ground to allow free movement of sand, favour its accumulation and regenerate the first bead of dunes beheaded.

In 2006 demolition process begins, award of new public tourist units, relocation and construction of beaches, backed by the city ordinance N° 2050/06. The project found favourable and adverse positions favouring the continuity of the same political team for a consecutive period of double government, and project manager of the waterfront redevelopment. A change of political ideology evident in the polls, introduced a different perception of the natural resource and printed a different look at the pace of construction of beach equipment, promoting the return of resorts built with cement.

The equipment and infrastructure of the beaches is marked by a succession of resorts built with wood, concrete, wood and ... again cement, so the scenario for the future and sustainability of the beach resorts is uncertain, as is also uncertain the management of coastal areas implemented by the local government.

The selected case study outlines the territorial transformations occurring in the environment, as well as the traces left by the antropia action. The town comes from an urbanization process that lacks a regulatory plan; it expands longitudinal and parallel to the coast, with their own manworks reflected in the multiple transformations of the territory being one of the root causes of environmental problems that the destination must overcome.

The origin and evolution of Villa Gesell tourism represents a clear example of the uncertainties in the processes of territorial development and the need to implement an integrated management of coastal areas based on responsible environmental attitude whose interests would prevail over economic issues, and independent of political ideology, they would reflect and act for the benefit of the natural resource, directing and controlling the coastal areas to ensure user satisfaction and preservation of the beach that sustains economic life of the town.

References

Barrado, D., & Calabuig, J. (2001). *World geography of tourism*. Madrid: Summaries.

Bevacqua, O. (2002). *Dr. Ing Heinrich Lömpel, Architect (1877-1951). His contribution in pioneering Villa Gesell – Museum Historical Archives of Villa Gesell*. Argentina: Printer Print S.C.

Callizo Soñeiro, J. (1991). *Approach to the geography of tourism*. Madrid: Summaries.

Gesell, R. (1983). *Carlos I. Gesell – His life*. Argentina: Copyright by Gesell Rosemarie Martinez Salas.

Lozato Giotart, J.P. (1990). *Geography of tourism – the space provided for the space consumed*. Barcelona: Masson Publishing.

Masor, O. (1975). *The history of Villa Gesell*. Argentina: Impressions Bariloche.

Oviedo, J.J. (2008). *Wealthy watering place: Poor people – A critical look at the Buenos Aires resorts*. Argentina: Graphics Printer.

Pallavecino, C., & Garcia, M.E. (2007). *Foundations of Villa Gesell. Museo Municipal Archives*. Argentina: Printer.

Pearce, D. (1988). *Tourism development – Planning and geographic location*. Mexico: Trillas.

Santos, M. (1990). *On a new geography*. Madrid: Escape Calpe.

—. (1997). *The nature of the space: Technical and time – Reason and emotion*. Barcelona: Ariel.

Sierra, D. (1969). *The tamer dunes*. Buenos Aires: Graphics Printer.

Strahler, A.N., & Strahler, A.H. (2005). *Physical geography*. Spain: Omega.

Tauber, F., Bognanni, L., & Delucci, D. (1998). *Villa Gesell reflections and data for a development strategy*. Argentina: National University of La Plata.

Vera Rebollo, F., López Palomeque, F., Marchena Gómez, M., & Anton Clave, S. (1997). *Territorial analysis of tourism. A new geography of tourism*. Barcelona: Ariel.

CHAPTER TWELVE

COLLABORATION AND RURAL DEVELOPMENT IN A TOURISM CONTEXT

PARHAD KEYIM

Abstract

Along with the changes and challenges encountered by the countryside, rural tourism is recognised as a useful development mechanism in terms of its socio–economic contribution. However, tourism's potential benefits for rural areas may depend upon rural development policies and practices that have been formulated and implemented in different socio–economic and institutional settings. The main purpose of this chapter is to outline a conceptual tourism collaboration approach modulated by the differing socio–economic and institutional rural settings of developed and developing countries. **Keywords:** collaborative tourism, rural development, institutional setting.

12.1. Introduction

Rural economies and societies around the world, whether in developed or developing countries, have faced major changes and challenges (Ashley & Maxwell, 2001; Gao, Huang, & Huang, 2009; OECD, 2006; Saarinen, 2007; Sharpley, 2007; Shortall & Shucksmith, 1998). These ongoing issues in rural areas have manifested in socio–economic problems such as the decline in employment and incomes, deterioration of amenities and services, and endangerment of ecosystems and landscapes. In this context, tourism in rural areas is recognised as a useful development mechanism in terms of its socio–economic contributions by creating local incomes and employment, reviving weakened amenities and services to residents, and aiding local cultural resource conservation (Hall & Jenkins, 1998). However, an absent or relatively little explored theme in previous studies is the dependence of rural tourism's potential benefits upon countryside development policies and practices (a collaboration approach in particular) that have been formulated and implemented in different socio–economic and institutional rural settings of developed and developing countries.

More specifically, the ideal tourism collaboration approach emphasises increasing the socio–economic contribution of tourism to rural areas (Bramwell & Sharman, 1999; Jamal & Getz, 1995; Selin & Chavez, 1995; Vernon, Essex, Pinder, & Curry, 2005). This is effected by encouraging non-hierarchical and flexible partnerships between the governmental (the public) and non-governmental (business, community and voluntary) sectors (Bramwell, 2011; Bramwell & Lane, 2011; Murdoch, 2000), encouraging bottom-up development and effectively mobilising the local human, cultural and natural resources. However, the feasibility and efficiency of this approach are dependent on the different socio–economic and institutional settings of rural areas. Against this backdrop the main goal of this chapter is to outline a conceptual tourism collaboration model that recognises the differing socio–economic and institutional rural settings of developed and developing countries.

12.2. Literature Review

Gray defines collaboration as "a process of joint decision making among key stakeholders of a problem domain about the future of that domain" (1989, p.227). The problem domain refers to a situation in which the problems are complex and require an inter- or multi-organisational response (Trist, 1983). Stakeholders are actors with an interest or stake in a common problem or issue and include all individuals, groups or organisations "directly influenced by the actions others take to solve a problem" (Gray, 1989, p.5). The concept of collaboration and/or similar concepts have been frequently applied to the fields of tourism and rural studies (Bramwell & Lane, 2011; Bramwell & Sharman, 1999; Cinneide & Burke, 1998; Jamal & Getz, 1995; Murdoch, 2000; Selin & Chavez, 1995; Vernon *et al.*, 2005).

The relationships between collaboration, tourism and development are rather complex and interconnected. Murdoch (2000) argues that because of a lack of binary thinking in terms of development, one needs to consider a 'network' (collaboration) approach that links the internal problems of rural areas with external opportunities. In this context, whereas exogenous (top-down) development is the result of outside forces (e.g. market forces and government policy), endogenous (bottom-up) development is the result of local initiatives.

Some scholars (Bramwell & Lane, 2011; Murdoch, 2000) maintain that governmental and non-governmental collaborations encourage bottom-up development, which increases the socio–economic contribution of tourism at the local rural (i.e. village) level. Bramwell (2011) claims that governance (i.e. governmental and non-governmental partnerships) is important for promoting sustainable development at tourist destinations. The state needs to redefine its role and to encourage the establishment of institutional architecture that supports co-operation and capacity building within and between governmental and non-governmental stakeholders. In other words, in order to avoid the pitfalls of marginal rural areas, external rural development agencies not only need to utilise their economic and political resources, but also to support the development of 'soft infrastructure' such as social capital, trust relations and learning capacities by including local actors.

Tourism in rural areas is recognised as a useful development mechanism (Cinneide & Burke, 1998; Murphy, 1988; Simmons, 1994). Rural tourism has been identified as a vehicle for regenerating the rural economy and maintaining rural ways of life (Lane, 1994). More concretely, tourism can contribute to rural areas in a socio–economic perspective by creating local income and employment, contributing local amenities and services, and aiding local cultural resource conservation (Hall & Jenkins, 1998).

However, the socio–economic contributions of tourism to rural areas may depend on countryside development policies and practices (a collaboration approach in particular) that have been formulated and implemented in different socio–economic and institutional settings. The ideal 'collaboration' approach emphasises the non-hierarchical and flexible alliance partnerships between governmental and non-governmental actors. However, the existence and feasibility of a 'collaboration' approach in situ (e.g. municipalities and villages) depends on the differing socio–economic and institutional settings of rural areas. Hall and Roberts argue that "…it is often difficult, and maybe impractical, to attempt to isolate the role of tourism from other dynamic social, economic and political processes in contributing to developmental outcomes" (2004, p.218). In other words, rural (tourism) development policy and practice need to be carried out through a 'collaboration' approach by means of governmental and non-governmental partnerships that are supposed to encourage bottom-up development and increase the socio–economic contribution of tourism in rural municipalities and villages.

12.3. A Conceptual Approach

The theoretical framework for this research draws primarily on Selin and Chavez's (1995) evolutionary tourism partnership model. They suggest that tourism collaboration progresses through five stages: antecedents, problem-setting, direction-setting, structuring and outcomes. Based on this evolutionary tourism partnership model, this research outlines a tourism collaboration approach that can be modulated by the differing socio–economic and institutional settings of rural areas within developed and developing countries (Table 12.1).

Table 12.1 – A collaboration process for rural tourism

Antecedents: Socio–economic and institutional settings of rural areas	
Collaboration stages	Description
Problem-setting	• Common problem identification: the changes and challenges in rural areas (problem domain), which are mainly manifested in socio–economic problems such as decline in employment and income, deterioration of rural amenities and services, and endangerment of rural ecosystems and landscapes, must be commonly identified by all stakeholders. • Recognition of interdependence: maximising the socio–economic contribution of tourism by all actors requires recognition of their interdependence. Because of the multiple stakeholders (i.e. the government, business, community and voluntary sectors) in the tourism industry, the problem domain requires collective action for its resolution and mutual agreement to ensure that the socio–economic benefits outweigh the costs of participation by each partner. • Involvement of broadly-based stakeholders: to avoid problems, rural development requires the involvement of all tourism–related stakeholders to combine and utilise local rural resilience (i.e. knowledge, expertise, and capital resources). • Consensus on legitimate/skilled convener: successful tourism collaboration requires common agreement among stakeholders concerning who has a legitimate stake (i.e. expertise, resources, and authority) in the collaboration issue.

Source: Selin & Chavez, 1995, p. 848; Jamal & Getz, 1995; OECD, 2006.

12.3.1. Contemporary socio–economic and institutional settings

Ashley and Maxwell (2001) have stated that rural areas are changing, particularly with respect to demography and diversification. More specifically:

- "Rural populations will stabilise while urban populations continue to grow rapidly. Will migration mean that rural areas lose their best young workers and become holding grounds for the very young and very old?" (2001, p.400).
- "Agriculture has declined sharply in relative terms, as an employer and as a contributor to exports and to GDP" (2001, p.398).
- "Most rural income in most places will be non-agricultural in origin (though with linkages to agriculture in many cases)" (2001, p.400).

If urbanisation causes the gradual reduction of social space in rural areas, it concurrently creates increasing demand for rural recreational spaces. The changing trends in rural areas stated above have created opportunities to establish rural recreational spaces in order to satisfy these urban demands and simultaneously provide employment for rural residents. Thus, as Baldock, Dwyer, Lowe, Petersen, and Ward (2001) claim, the countryside is perceived increasingly as a place for living and leisure instead of purely for 'production/consumption'. For example, rural hinterlands of economically advanced EU regions are increasingly being developed for tourism, second homes, retirement purposes, and nature protection.

In an institutional context, Jamal and Getz argue that "turbulence in the global environment of the 90s is driving the need to develop collaborative coping mechanisms different from the hierarchically structured forms of the traditional organisation" (1995, p.191). Shortall and Shuckmith suggest that "it is clear that the Commission and the European Parliament anticipate a fundamental change in support policies from a sectoral approach (agriculture) to one that is more territorial (rural)" (1998, p.74). More specifically, the socio–economic challenges of rural areas are recognised by the EU Commission and are reflected in its Cork Declaration of 1996. The Declaration aimed at "reversing rural out-migration, combating poverty, stimulating employment and equality of opportunity; and responding to growing requests for more quality, health, safety, personal development and leisure, and improved rural well-being". In order to achieve these goals, the Declaration proposed an integrated approach to be implemented in the form of a partnership among public, private and community interests (Shortall & Shucksmith, 1998). Integrated rural development emphasises the 'multifunctionality' of agriculture (rural areas), and supports various societal goals, including the creation of local rural incomes and employment, and maintenance of rural ecosystems and landscapes.

12.3.2. Problem-setting

Selin and Chavez emphasise that "in the problem-setting stage, the various interests begin to appreciate the interdependencies that exist among them and begin to realise that problem resolution will require collective action" (1995, p.849). In the context of tourism and rural development, the problem-setting phase of this conceptual collaboration approach mainly is focused on identifying the problem domain, recognising interdependence, the involvement of all stakeholders, and finding consensus on a legitimate/skilled convener.

Common problem identification: The changes and challenges in the contemporary rural world, whether in developed or developing countries, that mainly manifest in socio–economic problems, are well recognised (OECD, 2006; Sharpley, 2007). More specifically, the rural areas of developed Western countries are encountering regeneration problems. These problems are identified clearly by declining employment capacity, income and population, deteriorated rural amenities and services, and endangered rural ecosystems and landscapes affected by rural restructuring: in particular, the mechanisation of primary production and the 'harmonisation' of agriculture by European Union policy (Saarinen, 2007). Within developing countries, e.g. China, the rural development pace also is slowing as manifested in the growing income gap between urban and rural residents, and the prominent problem of relocation of extra rural labour, etc. These rural development issues in China are reduced to 'Three Nong' issues, namely agriculture, farmers, and rural areas (Gao *et al.*, 2009). In these contexts, tourism is recognised as a useful mechanism that can bring potential benefits to rural areas (Hall & Jenkins, 1998).

Recognition of interdependence: The character of the tourism industry with its multiple stakeholders (i.e. state, business, community and voluntary sectors) requires collective action in order to address the problem domain; it cannot be solved by a single actor (Cinneide & Burke, 1998). Specifically, mutual recognition of interdependence among stakeholders is required to maximise the socio–economic benefits of tourism for all actors. Additionally, common agreement among the stakeholders helps to ensure that the socio–economic benefits outweigh the costs of participation for each actor.

Involvement of broadly-based stakeholders: According to Gray, "successful collaboration depends on including a broad enough spectrum of stakeholders to mirror the critical components of the problem" (1989, p.68). Collaboration needs interactive work by cross-sectoral stakeholders on the problem domain in order to combine each actor's resilience (e.g. knowledge, expertise, and capital resources) to solve common problems (Vernon *et al.*, 2005). Tourism is a multiple stakeholder industry that is composed of multiple partner interests from the governmental and non-governmental sectors. Cinneide and Burke argue that "the coordinated development and marketing of tourism products requires the cooperation of product providers themselves and effective local and national partnerships between a range of private, public, and statutory stakeholders" (1998, p.305).

Further, the involvement of the various tourism stakeholders, especially community residents, is helpful for solving problems that appear during the implementation phase of tourism collaboration. De Araujo and Bramwell (2002) suggest that any restriction on participation by local communities, residents' associations, and other local interest groups affects all other aspects of regional tourism development policies and operation. Locals living in a tourist destination suffer the main impacts of tourism (Butler, 1980) and broader social development is achieved only when priority is given to the developmental needs and interests of local communities over the goals of the tourism industry (Brohman, 1996; Simmons, 1994).

However, the inclusion of broadly-based stakeholders during collaboration may depend on the socio–economic and institutional settings of the problem domain. In developed Western countries, the role of the public sector in tourism is limited to establishing a favourable development 'atmosphere' (e.g. political, regulatory, and economic) to enable tourism to flourish (Sharpley, 2008). Tourism-related decisions are usually made through inclusive partnerships among the governmental and non-governmental sectors. In developing countries, however, there are operational, structural, and cultural limitations to local communities' participation in tourism policymaking (Tosun, 2000). Tosun (2000) demonstrates that complex government bureaucracies fragment the planning process and obstruct coordinated policymaking. In some developing countries, there is a lack of opportunities for rural community residents to participate in local decision-making. Additionally, rural residents often have minimal experience of democracy (i.e. bottom-up decision-making and development). For example, in China the government plays the dominant role in tourism development, acting as planner, investor, investment stimulator, promoter, educator, and regulator (Keyim, 2012; Qin, Wall, & Liu, 2011). Thus, rural (tourism) development policy and practice emphasise the state's dominant role without sufficiently considering other rural development actors that include local rural community residents (Bao & Sun, 2007; Keyim, 2012; Li, 2004; Li, Lai, & Feng, 2007). Rural residents in China are in a relatively inferior position among tourism stakeholders, since procedures that guarantee citizens the right to participate in public decision-making before, during, and after an event are not yet established as they are in Western societies (Bao & Sun, 2007).

Consensus on legitimate/skilled convener: Collaboration requires common agreement among stakeholders concerning who has a legitimate stake in the issue. Pearce, Moscardo, and Ross (1996) highlight five prerequisites to participation: legal rights and opportunities to participate, access to information, provision of enough resources for people or groups to get involved, and being genuinely public, which is broad instead of selective, and involvement from the concerned communities. Bramwell and Sharman argue that "concern for the important systemic constraints which affect collaboration is integrated with the need to identify whether there is evidence of more democratic forms of policymaking" (1999, p.395). Partnerships may be more successful when they are led by a convener who is perceived as having legitimacy, expertise, resources, and authority and for this reason can be a government agency, industrial firm, or group (e.g. local Chamber of Commerce, tourist firm, LEADER organisation) (Jamal & Getz, 1995; Parker, 2000).

However, Murdoch and Abram (1998) counter that in a certain policy sector the state still needs to impose a 'dominant strategic line' since it usually dominates economic and political resources. In other words, the government should attract new external industries in order to solve the problems of marginality and backwardness of rural areas by utilising its economic and political resources (e.g. relatively advanced skills, experience, and preferential policy for land allocation and tax). Edwards, Goodwin, Pemberton, and Woods (2001) emphasise that although the responsibility of local state authorities has shifted to 'partnership' governance that is composed of a wider range of actors, 'partnership committees' remain dominated by state sector representatives, who steer partnership working, promote partnerships in policy documentation, and instigate, fund and resource partnerships. The lack of community ownership, capital, skills, knowledge and resources, as pointed out by Scheyvens (1999), constrains the countryside's ability to fully control its participation in tourism development. In the Chinese vertical bureaucratic system, the government and its 'business-bureaucracy collaboration' partner (e.g. external enterprises) have become the legitimate convener of rural (tourism) development, as they control the necessary ingredients for such development including policies, funds, community resources, land and local cultural heritage (Li *et al.*, 2007). Also, Ying and Zhou argue that "in fact, China's current vertical bureaucratic system, which lacks a clear definition of governments' respective purviews and commitments in administration, enables the governments to intervene into the rural cultural tourism development to an optional extent, according to their practical interests and needs" (2007, p.104).

12.3.3. Direction-setting

The direction-setting phase of collaboration focuses on the achievement of 'policy consensus' (Vernon *et al.*, 2005) among stakeholders on the solution of the problem domain. In other words, it emphasises the collective in the deeper exploration and negotiation of the problem by members and their intention to reach agreement.

Goal establishment: Within challenged rural areas, tourism is identified and appreciated as a socio–economic development mechanism. However, tourism's perceived role in this development may be appreciated differently in different socio-political settings (socio–economic and institutional context). That is to say, although the developed Western world is interested in the economic benefits of tourism for rural areas, it also considers the negative socio-cultural impacts. However, developing countries, such as China, mainly focus on the economic benefits of tourism in rural areas (e.g. creating income and employment) but overlook the negative socio–cultural impacts (Bao & Sun, 2007; Yang & Wall, 2008). Thus, one needs to consider the multiple interests of different stakeholders during collaboration. Otherwise, the 'economy priority' aim of a rural (tourism) development strategy in developing countries could lead to the flourishing of 'business-bureaucracy collaboration' (Keyim, 2012; Li *et al.*, 2007) at the expense of more inclusive collaboration that includes the governmental and non-governmental sectors.

Basic role establishment: Maximising and/or evenly distributing the socio–economic contribution of tourism to rural areas requires the encouragement of non-hierarchical and flexible alliances, partnerships among tourism-related government and non-government stakeholders. In other words, collaboration not only requires the involvement of all stakeholders but also non-hierarchical and flexible alliances among them. Vernon *et al.* argue that "incomplete representation, unequal power relations of stakeholders, or lack of accountability can weaken the effectiveness of policies and initiatives" (2005, p.329). Jamal and Getz suggest that "a stakeholder who is impacted by the actions of other stakeholders has a right to become involved in order to moderate those impacts, but must also have the resources and skills (capacity) in order to participate" (1995, p.194). Thus, the participation of non–governmental stakeholders must be encouraged by strengthening their development-related capacities, including vocational skills and financial resources, decision-making, and implementing power (Keyim, 2012).

12.3.4. Structuring (implementation)

The structuring (implementation) phase of collaboration involves institutionalising the shared meanings of the group and devising a regulatory framework to guide future collective action (Gray, 1985).

Formalising relationships: Theoretically the ideal collaboration should be established among the various government and non-government stakeholders on an equal power basis. However, in practice the power of stakeholders is often unequal: "power governs the interaction of individuals, organisations and agencies influencing, or trying to influence, the formulation of tourism policy and the manner in which it is implemented" (Hall, 1994, p.52). Similarly, Bramwell and Sharman note that because of the power imbalance between stakeholders "collaborative arrangements in destinations can become conversations among local elites, rather than involving a representative range of stakeholders" (1999, p.396). The views of powerful participants (e.g. elites such as the government) may prevail in collaboration if sustained attention is not paid to the interests, values, and attitudes of all participants (Joppe, 1996). Yang and Wall (2008) argue that insufficient planning supervision in China has led to many problems, such as power abuse and corruption, and local tourism planning can become a tool to satisfy power holders and business interests at the expense of public benefits. Thus, the collaboration convener (usually the government) needs to step back to encourage collective decision-making and consensus-building in order to intensify participation (Robinson, 1997). In other words, the public sector needs to act as a 'provider' rather than an 'enabler' during collaborative policymaking by encouraging more 'bottom-up', decentralised, and inclusive forms of governance that would allow local communities and businesses to take more responsibility (Vernon *et al.*, 2005) and maximise the socio–economic contribution of tourism to the local rural community.

Adequate resources for collaboration: Jamal and Getz (1995) suggest that sufficient resources, including expertise, time, and money, are needed to ensure the progress of collaboration. Scott (2004) argues that various stakeholders do not have the necessary resources to handle the multi-dimensional nature of the rural development problem. The partnership process itself requires investment for capacity-building and skill development of partners, especially for the most marginalised, weaker, and less-experienced interests in the community. Citing Putnam (1993), Shortall and Shuckmith (1998) contend that the essence of 'capacity building' is the creation of social capital of various forms that could benefit the whole community. Leadership and other skills, organisational and physical infrastructure, partnership and co-ordination, community confidence and identity, entrepreneurship, networks, trust, and even social cohesion are all examples of the social capital that can be created or enhanced through such an approach. Murdoch and Abram (1998) argue that the limitation of community residents during partnership work, caused perhaps by a lack of abilities or resources, requires the government to emphasise an 'exogenous development' approach in order to protect the least active residents and communities. The government also needs to encourage 'endogenous development' for the best use of existing rural resources that are critical to rural development. In other words, grass–roots 'bottom–up' development practices should be encouraged in order to solve some critical problems such as over–reliance on state support, dependence on single–sector large firms, and marginalisation of small–scale local enterprises. Local tacit knowledge can also be utilised as a resource for local capacity-building.

12.4. Conclusion

Based on Selin and Chavez's (1995) evolutionary tourism partnership model, which progresses through stages of antecedents, problem-setting, direction-setting, structuring, and outcomes, this article outlines a tourism collaboration approach that can be modulated by the differing socio–economic and institutional settings of rural areas within developed and developing countries. These tourism collaboration phases are interconnected and, as Vernon *et al.* (2005) claim, the overall effectiveness of collaboration will be determined by influences in each of the collaboration phases.

According to this framework, resolving the common socio–economic problems that are caused by the changes and challenges in rural areas of the developed and developing world requires collaboration between the governmental and non-governmental (business, community, and voluntary) sectors in the form of non-hierarchical and flexible alliances and partnerships. In this context, tourism collaboration begins with the problem-setting stage that is initiated through an appreciation of the challenges by rural (tourism) development–related stakeholders. The recognition of the interdependence and broader involvement of stakeholders from all sectors is required at this stage in order to combine and utilise the resilience of the various stakeholders and to prevent problems during the implementation phase of tourism collaboration. However, the inclusion of broadly-based stakeholders during collaboration, which is best led by a legitimate and skilled convener, is modulated by the differing socio–economic and institutional settings of rural areas within developed and developing countries. In other words, the representativeness of various stakeholders during tourism collaboration needs to be considered in differing socio–economic and institutional contexts of rural areas in developed and developing countries.

Subsequently, the direction–setting phase of collaboration will be introduced through the identification and appreciation of tourism as a socio–economic development mechanism by all the rural development-related stakeholders. However, this perceived goal of tourism development in rural areas might be set differently in the various socio–economic and institutional settings of developed and developing countries. At this stage of collaboration the involvement of the various stakeholders from all sectors, especially the involvement of community stakeholders, for the purpose of maximising and evenly distributing the socio–economic contribution of tourism to rural areas can be modulated by differing socio–economic and institutional settings.

Finally, the structuring or implementation phase of tourism collaboration requires construction of a suitable structure for institutionalising the tourism and rural development process that supports the maximisation of its socio–economic contribution to the local rural community. It needs to establish a broader and equal partnership between governmental and non–governmental stakeholders, especially concerning decision-making and implementing power, in order to advocate the representativeness of stakeholders with different backgrounds. However, the broader involvement of stakeholders from all sectors during all phases of the tourism collaboration approach, especially the involvement of community stakeholders, is modulated by differing socio–economic and institutional rural settings within developed and developing countries. This all-inclusive tourism collaboration approach requires adequate resources to ensure the implementation of collaboration through the provision of external and/or internal mandates, including initial government investment in community capacity–building and encouragement of 'bottom–up' development.

Overall, the problem-setting, direction-setting, and structuring phases of the collaboration approach, which are interconnected in the context of tourism and rural development, are modulated by the differing socio–economic and institutional settings of rural areas within developed and developing countries. Thus, the outcomes of tourism collaboration, which are seen to have a more positive than negative impact, are also affected by the differing socio–economic and institutional settings of rural areas. This study merely attempts to investigate tourism collaboration in a rural context through a conceptual approach; it would be worth conducting empirical research within socio–economic and institutional rural settings in different countries in order to prove the feasibility and efficiency of tourism collaboration in these contexts.

Acknowledgements

The author thanks the Kyösti Haataja Foundation (project no – 201410017) for its financial support. Special thanks to Paul Fryer for his improvement of the manuscript.

References

Ashley, C., & Maxwell, S. (2001). Rethinking rural development. *Development Policy Review, 19*(4), 395-425.

Baldock, D., Dwyer, J., Lowe, P., Petersen, J.E., & Ward, N. (2001). *The nature of rural development: Towards a sustainable integrated rural policy in Europe.* London: Institute for European Environmental Policy.

Bao, J.G., & Sun, J.X. (2007). Differences in community participation in tourism development between China and the West. *Chinese Sociology & Anthropology, 39*(3), 9-27.

Bramwell, B. (2011). Governance, the state and sustainable tourism: A political economy approach. *Journal of Sustainable Tourism, 19*(4-5), 459-477.

Bramwell, B., & Lane, B. (2011). Critical research on the governance of tourism and sustainability. *Journal of Sustainable Tourism, 19*(4-5), 411-421.

Bramwell, B., & Sharman, A. (1999). Collaboration in local tourism policymaking. *Annals of Tourism Research, 26*(2), 392-415.

Brohman, J. (1996). New directions in tourism for third world development. *Annals of Tourism Research, 23*(1), 48-70.

Butler, R.W. (1980). The concept of a tourist area cycle of evolution: implications for management of resources. *The Canadian Geographer, 24*(1), 5-12.

Cinneide, M., & Burke, J. (1998). The development of community-based rural tourism in Ireland. In C. Neil, & M. Tykkyläinen (eds.). *Local economic development: A geographical comparison of rural community restructuring* (pp. 209-306). Tokyo: United Nations University Press.

De Araujo, L.M., & Bramwell, B. (2002). Partnership and regional tourism in Brazil. *Annals of Tourism Research, 29*(4), 1138-1164.

Edwards, B., Goodwin, M., Pemberton, S., & Woods, M. (2001). Partnerships, power, and scale in rural governance. *Environment and Planning C, 19*(2), 289-310.

Gao, S., Huang, S., & Huang, Y. (2009). Rural tourism development in China. *International Journal of Tourism Research, 11*(5), 439-450.

Gray, B. (1985). Conditions facilitating interorganizational collaboration. *Human Relations, 38*(10), 911- 936.

—. (1989). *Collaborating: Finding common ground for multiparty problems.* San Francisco, CA: Jossey-Bass Press.

Hall, C.M. (1994). *Tourism and politics: policy, power and place.* Chichester: John Wiley.

Hall, D., & Roberts, L. (2004). Conclusions and future agenda. In D. Hall (Ed.), *Tourism and transition: Governance, transformation, and development* (pp. 217-227). Trowbridge: Cromwell Press.

Hall, M., & Jenkins, J. (1998). The policy dimensions of rural tourism and recreation. In R. Butler, M. Hall, & J. Jenkins (eds.). *Tourism and recreation in rural areas* (pp.19-42). Chichester: John Wiley.

Jamal, T.B., & Getz, D. (1995). Collaboration theory and community tourism planning. *Annals of Tourism Research, 22*(1), 186-204.

Joppe, M. (1996). Sustainable community tourism development revisited. *Tourism Management, 17*(7), 475-479.

Keyim, P. (2012). Government roles in rural tourism development: a case from Turpan. *Tourism Today, 12*, 113-133.

Lane, B. (1994). What is rural tourism? *Journal of Sustainable Tourism, 2*(1-2), 7-21.

Li, Y. (2004). Exploring community tourism in China. *Journal of Sustainable Tourism, 12*(3), 175-193.

Li, Y., Lai, K., & Feng, X. (2007). The problem of 'Guanxi' for actualizing community tourism: A case study of relationship networking in China. *Tourism Geographies, 9*(2), 115-138.

Murdoch, J. (2000). Networks—a new paradigm of rural development? *Journal of Rural Studies, 16*(4), 407-419.

Murdoch, J., & Abram, S. (1998). Defining the limits of community governance. *Journal of Rural Studies, 14*(1), 41-50.

Murphy, P.E. (1988). Community driven tourism planning. *Tourism Management, 9*(2), 96-104.

OECD (2006). *The new rural paradigm: Policies and governance.* Paris: OECD.

Parker, S. (2000). Collaboration on tourism policy making: Environmental and commercial sustainability on Bonaire, NA. In B. Bramwell, & B. Lane (eds.). *Tourism collaboration and partnerships: Politics, practice and sustainability* (pp. 78-97). Clevedon: Channel View.

Pearce, P.L., Moscardo, G.M., & Ross, G.F. (1996). *Tourism community relationships.* Oxford: Pergamon.

Qin, Q., Wall, G., & Liu, X. (2011). Government roles in stimulating tourism development: A case from Guangxi, China. *Asia Pacific Journal of Tourism Research, 16*(5), 471-487.

Robinson, G.M. (1997). Community-based planning: Canada's Atlantic coastal action program (ACAP). *Geographical Journal, 163*(1), 25-37.

Saarinen, J. (2007). Contradictions of rural tourism initiatives in rural development contexts: Finnish rural tourism strategy case study. *Current Issues in Tourism, 10*(1), 96-105.

Scheyvens, R. (1999). Ecotourism and the empowerment of local communities. *Tourism Management, 20*(2), 245-249.

Scott, M. (2004). Building institutional capacity in rural Northern Ireland: the role of partnership governance in the LEADER II programme. *Journal of Rural Studies, 20*(1), 49-59.

Selin, S., & Chavez, D. (1995). Developing an evolutionary tourism partnership model. *Annals of Tourism Research, 22*(4), 844-856.

Sharpley, R. (2007). Flagship attractions and sustainable rural tourism development. *Journal of Sustainable Tourism, 15*(2), 125-143.

—. (2008). Planning for tourism: The case of Dubai. *Tourism and Hospitality Planning & Development, 5*(1), 13-30.

Shortall, S., & Shucksmith, M. (1998). Integrated rural development: issues arising from the Scottish experience. *European Planning Studies, 6*(1), 73-88.

Simmons, D.G. (1994). Community participation in tourism planning. *Tourism Management, 15*(2), 98-108.

Tosun, C. (2000). Limits to community participation in the tourism development process in developing countries. *Tourism Management*, *21*(6), 613-633.

Trist, E. (1983). Referent organizations and the development of inter-organizational domains. *Human Relations*, *36*(3), 269-284.

Vernon, J., Essex, S., Pinder, D., & Curry, K. (2005). Collaborative policymaking: Local sustainable projects. *Annals of Tourism Research*, *32*(2), 325-345.

Yang, L., & Wall, G. (2008). The evolution and status of tourism planning: Xishuangbanna, Yunnan, China. *Tourism and Hospitality Planning & Development*, *5*(2), 165-182.

Ying, T., & Zhou, Y. (2007). Community, governments and external capitals in China's rural cultural tourism: A comparative study of two adjacent villages. *Tourism Management*, *28*(1), 96-107.

INDEX